I0109705

Mike McGrath

Perl
Programming

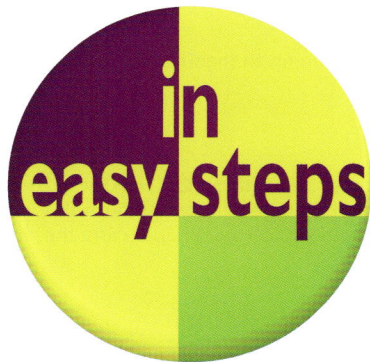

in
easy steps

Second edition

In easy steps is an imprint of In Easy Steps Limited
16 Hamilton Terrace · Holly Walk · Leamington Spa
Warwickshire · United Kingdom · CV32 4LY
www.ineasysteps.com

Second edition

Copyright © 2025 by In Easy Steps Limited. All rights reserved. No part
of this book may be reproduced or transmitted in any form or by any
means, electronic or mechanical, including photocopying, recording,
or by any information storage or retrieval system, without prior
written permission from the publisher.

Notice of Liability
Every effort has been made to ensure that this book contains accurate
and current information. However, In Easy Steps Limited and the
author shall not be liable for any loss or damage suffered by readers
as a result of any information contained herein.

Trademarks
All trademarks are acknowledged as belonging to their respective
companies.

In Easy Steps Limited supports The Forest Stewardship Council (FSC),
the leading international forest certification organization. All our titles
that are printed on Greenpeace approved FSC certified paper carry the
FSC logo.

FSC
www.fsc.org

MIX
Paper from
responsible sources
FSC® C020837

Printed and bound in the United Kingdom

ISBN 978-1-78791-048-5

Contents

Index   187

The examples in this book demonstrate features of the Perl programming language and the screenshots illustrate the actual results produced by executing the listed code examples.

Certain colorization conventions are used to clarify the code listed in the steps. Perl keywords are colored blue, variables are orange, numeric values are red, code comments are green, general program code is black.

For example...

```perl
use strict ;
use warnings ;
# Output a range of numbers.
my @arr = (1..12) ;
print "One Dozen: @arr \n" ;
```

script.pl   module.pm   page.html

To easily identify the source code for the example programs described in the steps, a file icon and file name appears in the margin alongside the steps:

For convenience, the source code files from all examples featured in this book are available in a single ZIP archive. Visit **www.ineasysteps.com** and log in, then navigate to Free Resources and click the Browse Now button in the Source code downloads and other book resources section, and select the Perl code examples item. Extract the archive contents to a handy location on your computer to try the examples.

The screenshots in this book illustrate the actual results of executing the listed code steps. If you don't achieve the result illustrated in any example, simply compare your code to that in the original example files you have downloaded to discover where you went wrong.

1 Getting Started

Welcome to the exciting world of Perl programming. This chapter demonstrates how to create Perl programs and how to store reusable data in scalar, array, and hash variables.

The Perl Foundation is dedicated to advancing the Perl programming language. Discover more at **perlfoundation.org**

Introducing Perl

Perl is a high-level general purpose programming language that runs on over 100 platforms. Originally developed by Larry Wall back in 1987, Perl has since undergone many changes and revisions to become suitable for both rapid prototyping and for large-scale development projects.

Perl began as a Unix scripting language to make report processing easier. Its name is therefore sometimes thought to represent the title "Practical Extraction and Reporting Language", although it is not officially an acronym.

Perl Features

- **Compatibility** – Perl runs on various operating systems including Windows, Linux, and macOS.

- **Clarity** – Perl is easy to read and write, making it popular with beginners and experts alike.

- **Execution** – Perl programs are executed directly by its interpreter, without creating a portable executable file.

- **Text Handling** – Perl contains tools for processing text, including HTML, XML, and other markup languages.

- **Pattern Matching** – Perl supports Regular Expressions for text manipulation.

- **Universality** – Perl supports Unicode characters for international text processing.

- **Flexibility** – Perl supports procedural, object-oriented, and functional programming paradigms.

- **Extensibility** – Perl provides access to over 25,000 modules via the Comprehensive Perl Archive Network (CPAN).

- **Integration** – Perl supports third-party databases, such as MySQL, via its database integration interface (DBI).

- **Connection** – Perl can interface with external C/C++ libraries via its XS and SWIG tools.

- **Accessibility** – Perl is Open Source software, licensed under its Artistic License or the General Public License (GPL).

The power and versatility of Perl has earned it the reputation as the Swiss Army Knife of programming languages. It used to be the most popular web programming language, so was often also referred to as "the duct tape of the Internet".

Perl and the Web

- Perl's text manipulation capabilities and rapid development cycle make it an ideal web programming language.

- There are many web frameworks written in Perl, such as the "Catalyst" model-view-controller (MVC) framework.

- CPAN provides Perl modules for almost any task, from URL or image manipulation to web API (Application Programming Interface) interaction.

- Perl's DBI module makes it easy to integrate with web databases for data storage and retrieval.

- Many large web-based applications are written solely in Perl.

- Perl can securely handle encrypted web data, including e-commerce transactions.

- Perl can be embedded into web servers for speedy processing.

Perl Interpretation

The Perl interpreter executes programs in several stages, to ensure efficient processing and execution:

- **Parsing** – The interpreter reads a program and parses it into an internal syntax tree. The tree is checked for syntax errors, then the interpreter optimizes it for better performance.

- **Execution** – The optimized syntax tree is converted into bytecode, which is then executed. The interpreter dynamically determines data types and handles memory management.

- **Runtime** – The interpreter loads any required external modules and libraries, and adapts the program according to context. Runtime errors are caught and reported.

Everything relating to the Perl programming language can be found on the official Perl website at **perl.org**

Hot tip

Unix/Linux and macOS users who do not have Perl can scroll down this web page for links to download Perl for their respective systems.

Installing Perl

In order to execute Perl programs it is, of course, necessary to have Perl installed on your system. Happily, all modern versions of the Unix, Linux, and macOS operating systems have Perl installed by default. To confirm you do indeed have Perl on your system, simply open a Terminal window and enter the command **perl -v**. If present, Perl will respond with something like this:

```
File  Edit  View  Search  Terminal  Help
mike@LinuxPC:~$ perl -v

This is perl 5, version 40, built for x86_64-linux-gnu-thread-multi
Copyright 1987-2025, Larry Wall

Perl may be copied only under the terms of either the Artistic License or the
GNU General Public License, which may be found in the Perl 5 source kit.

Complete documentation for Perl, including FAQ lists, should be found on
this system using "man perl" or "perldoc perl".  If you have access to the
Internet, point your browser at https://www.perl.org/, the Perl Home Page.

mike@LinuxPC:~$
```

Windows users will need to download and install Perl before they can continue on their Perl adventure:

1 Launch a web browser, then navigate to the official "Perl Download" page at **www.perl.org/get.html**

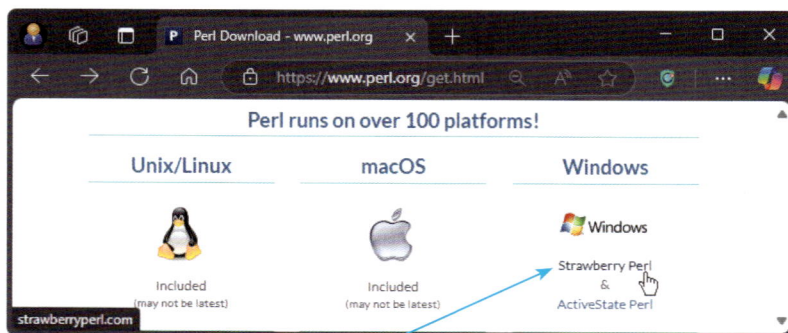

2 Select the "Strawberry Perl" link to be taken to the download page of the free community edition of Perl

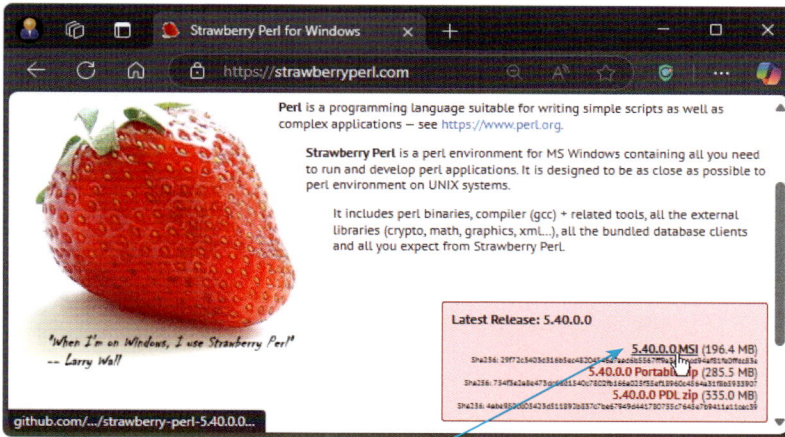

MSI Installer

3 Next, select the Microsoft Installer (MSI) link to download the Strawberry Perl setup installer

4 When download is complete, launch the Strawberry Perl installer, accept the license terms, then click **Next**

5 Choose **C:** as the "Destination Folder" then click **Next**, **Install**, and **Yes** to agree the "User Account" dialog

6 When installation is complete, click **Finish** to end setup

7 To confirm you now have Perl on your system, open a Command Prompt/Terminal window and enter the command **perl -v** to see Perl respond something like this

```
C:\Users\mike_>perl -v

This is perl 5, version 40, built for MSWin32-x64-multi-thread
Copyright 1987-2025, Larry Wall

Perl may be copied only under the terms of either the Artistic License or the
GNU General Public License, which may be found in the Perl 5 source kit.

Complete documentation for Perl, including FAQ lists, should be found on
this system using "man perl" or "perldoc perl".  If you have access to the
Internet, point your browser at https://www.perl.org/, the Perl Home Page.

C:\Users\mike_>
```

11

Hot tip

To open a Command Prompt window, you can press the **WinKey** + **R** keys to launch a "Run" dialog, then type **cmd** into the dialog and click **OK**.

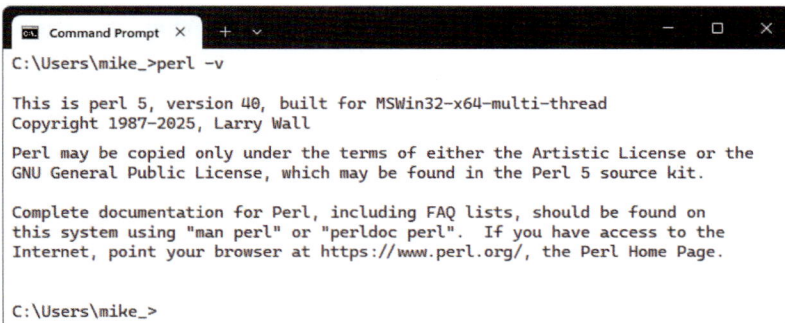

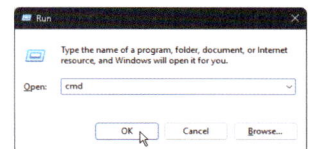

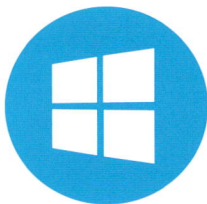

Scripting on Windows

Perl programs are simply textual "script" files that can be created in any plain text editor such as Windows' Notepad application. Each Perl script file must be given a name of your choice followed by a **.pl** or **.PL** file extension. It's useful to create a folder (directory) in which to store your Perl scripts. Follow these steps to create a Perl program that will output a traditional greeting:

1 Open a Command Prompt/Terminal window and create a new folder in which to store Perl scripts. For example, make a subdirectory named "Scripts" in the root directory **mkdir C:\Scripts**

2 Open a plain text editor, such as Notepad, and precisely copy this Perl code into the text editor
```
# Output the traditional greeting.
print "Hello World! \n" ;
```

hello.pl

3 Save the file in your scripts folder, named as "hello.pl"

4 Next, in the Command Prompt/Terminal window, change directory to your scripts folder, for example enter **cd C:\Scripts**

5 Now, at the prompt, enter this command to call upon the Perl interpreter to execute the program **perl hello.pl**

6 See the traditional greeting is now output in the Command Prompt/Terminal window

```
C:\Users\mike_>mkdir C:\Scripts

C:\Users\mike_>cd C:\Scripts

C:\Scripts>perl hello.pl
Hello World!

C:\Scripts>_
```

Individual parts of the "hello.pl" program script on the opposite page can be examined in order to better understand the code:

Comments

● **# Output the traditional greeting.**

The first line is an explanatory single-line "comment". Everything on the line following the **#** character is completely ignored by the Perl interpreter. Comments are useful to help explain your code to others, or to yourself when revisiting the code later. Multiline comments can be included outside of executable code like this:

=pod
This is a multiline comment in Plain Old Documentation (POD).
Everything is ignored until the Perl interpreter meets the =cut line.
=cut

Functions

● **print**

The second line begins by calling the Perl **print** function to output content (its "argument"). Function calls in other programming languages, such as Python, are typically followed by **( )** parentheses that contain function arguments, such as **print("Hello World!\n");** Optionally, the parentheses can be omitted in Perl function calls.

Strings

● **"Hello World! \n"**

Text strings in Perl must be enclosed in quote marks. You may use single quote marks or double quote marks, but these have different behaviors. Double quotes, as used here, allow "interpolation", which translates special escape sequences – such as **\n** to output a new line and **\t** to output a tab space. Single quote marks simply treat the string literally and output all characters between the quotes.

Statements

● **print "Hello World! \n" ;**

The entire second line is a "statement". All statements in Perl must be terminated with a ; semicolon character – just as all sentences in the English language must end with a full stop.

Hot tip

You can send multiple items to the **print** function as a comma-separated list. The **print** function will process them in turn and output them sequentially.

13

Hot tip

Perl code should not include unnecessary spaces. So, the statement should be written as **print "Hello World!\n";** but spaces are added in this book's listed example code for clarity.

Scripting on Linux

Perl programs are simply textual "script" files that can be created in any plain text editor, such as the vi or xed text editors. Each Perl script file must be given a name of your choice followed by a **.pl** or **.PL** file extension. It's useful to create a folder (directory) in which to store your Perl scripts. Follow these steps to create a Perl program that will output a traditional greeting:

1 Open a Terminal window and create a new folder in which to store Perl scripts. For example, make a subdirectory named "Scripts" in the home directory
mkdir ~/Scripts

2 Next, in the Terminal window, change directory into your scripts folder – for example, enter
cd ~/Scripts

greet.pl

3 Open a plain text editor, such as vi or xed, and precisely copy this Perl code into the text editor
 # Output the traditional greeting.
print "Hello World! \n" ;

4 Save the file in your scripts folder, named as "greet.pl"

5 Now, at the prompt, enter this command to call upon the Perl interpreter to execute the program
perl hello.pl

6 See the traditional greeting is now output in the Terminal window

Don't forget

This book uses Windows to demonstrate examples, as it's the most commonly used operating system.

```
mike@LinuxPC: ~/Scripts
File  Edit  View  Search  Terminal  Help
mike@LinuxPC:~$ mkdir ~/Scripts
mike@LinuxPC:~$ cd ~/Scripts
mike@LinuxPC:~/Scripts$ vi
mike@LinuxPC:~/Scripts$ perl greet.pl
Hello World!
mike@LinuxPC:~/Scripts$ 
```

Optionally, Perl programs in Unix-based operating systems can be made executable by adding the path to the Perl interpreter in a special **#!** "shebang line" at the start of the script, and by changing the file permissions.

7 Open the "greet.pl" program file in your text editor and add this line at the very start of the script
#!/usr/bin/perl

8 Save the modified file – which can now find the Perl interpreter on your system

9 Next, return to the Terminal window and give yourself read, write, and execute permission and allow other users to read and execute the program in this script file
chmod 0755 greet.pl

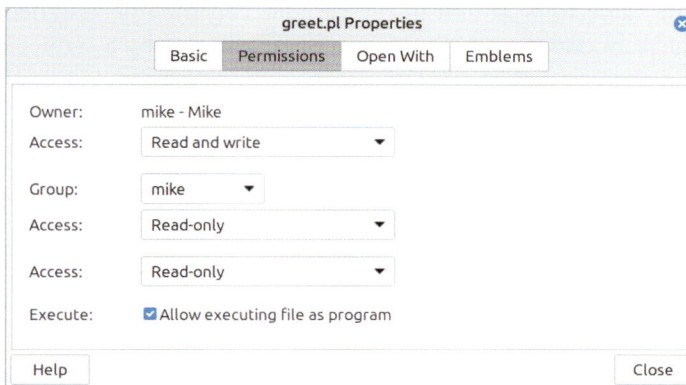

greet.pl Properties			⊗
Basic	**Permissions**	Open With	Emblems

Owner:	mike - Mike
Access:	Read and write ▼
Group:	mike ▼
Access:	Read-only ▼
Access:	Read-only ▼
Execute:	☑ Allow executing file as program

Help		Close

10 Now, at the prompt, enter this command to execute the program and see the greeting output once more
./greet.pl

```
                    mike@LinuxPC: ~/Scripts              _ □ ⊗
File  Edit  View  Search  Terminal  Help
mike@LinuxPC:~/Scripts$ chmod 0755 greet.pl
mike@LinuxPC:~/Scripts$ ./greet.pl
Hello World!
mike@LinuxPC:~/Scripts$ ▊
```

15

The shebang line is so-named as a contraction of the character names # (sharp) and ! (bang).

Storing values

A "variable" is like a container in a Perl program in which a data value can be stored inside the computer's memory. The stored value can be referenced using the variable's name.

The programmer can choose any name for a variable, providing it adheres to the Perl naming conventions – the name may only contain letters, digits, and the underscore character, but typically will begin with a letter or underscore. The Perl keywords, listed on the inside cover of this book, must also be avoided. There are three types of variable in Perl programming:

● **Scalar** – able to store a single number, string, or reference.

● **Array** – able to store an ordered list of scalars.

● **Hash** – able to store an unordered set of keys/value pairs.

A scalar variable is created with a **$** dollar symbol, followed by a name of your choice (adhering to the Perl naming conventions). The value to be stored in the variable can then be assigned using the **=** operator, and the statement terminated by a semicolon:

$*scalar_variable_name* **=** *value* ;

Perl automatically determines the data type based on the value assigned to the variable and provides an appropriate amount of memory for numbers and strings.

There is no dedicated Boolean data type in Perl, but true and false values are determined based on the context of the value:

False Values	
0	The number zero.
'0'	A string containing only the digit zero.
"	An empty string.
undef	An undefined value.
( )	An empty list.
True Values	
Any non-zero number (e.g. **1**, **-1**, **3.14**).	
Any non-empty string (e.g. **'true'**).	
Arrays, objects, references.	

Beware

Perl is case-sensitive, so **$var**, **$Var**, and **$VAR** are seen as three distinct variables – use only lowercase for your variable names.

Hot tip

It's good practice to choose meaningful names to make the code more comprehensible and to use "snake_case" for lengthy variable names – all lowercase, and words separated by an underscore character.

Different values, of any data type, can be assigned to a variable as the program proceeds. Whitespace contained within an assigned string will be preserved in output.

Literal strings can best be assigned to variables by enclosing the string in single quote marks. Double quotes can, however, be used for output as interpolation can translate variable names into the value they contain, in addition to translating escape characters.

1 Open a plain text editor and create a scalar variable containing a literal string value
```perl
$var = 'World' ;
```

2 Next, output the variable value using interpolation
```perl
print "\nHello $var! \n" ;
```

3 Now, assign a new string value to the scalar variable, then output it in a string containing leading whitespace
```perl
$var = 'Europe' ;
print "     Hello $var \n" ;
```

4 Then, assign another string to the scalar variable, and output it in a string with a tab space but no final newline
```perl
$var = "America, Population:" ;
print "\tHello $var" ;
```

5 Finally, assign a numeric value to the scalar variable, then output it in a string
```perl
$var = 342 ;
print "$var Million \n" ;
```

6 Save the file in your scripts folder, named as "scalar.pl", then, at a Terminal prompt, execute the program
```
perl scalar.pl
```

scalar.pl

Hot tip

You can actually enclose literal strings within double quotes, but using single quotes instead enables the code to run faster as the interpreter need not then check for any required interpolation substitution.

17

```
Command Prompt    +  ∨                    —  □  ✕

C:\Scripts>perl scalar.pl

Hello World!
    Hello Europe
        Hello America, Population:342 Million
```

Employing arrays

An "array" is a variable that can store multiple items of data – unlike a scalar variable, which can only store one piece of data. The pieces of data are stored sequentially in array "elements" that can be referenced by a zero-based index (starting at 0). The first value in element 0; the second value in element 1; and so on.

An array variable is declared in the same way as a scalar variable, but an array name is prefixed by an @ symbol. Values are assigned to the array elements as a comma-separated list within parentheses. For example, the syntax to declare an array named "nums" to store six scalar numbers looks like this:

```
@nums = ( 1, 2, 3, 4, 5, 6 ) ;
```

The entire array can be referenced just by the array name – in this case by **@nums**. An individual element can be referenced using the array name prefixed by a **$** character and followed by square brackets containing the element number. This means that **$nums[1]** references the second element in the example above – not the first element, as element numbering starts at 0.

Arrays in Perl can contain a mixture of numbers and strings as each element can contain any scalar value. There is also a shortcut to assign sequential numbers and letters using a .. range operator:

```
@dozen = ( 1..12 ) ;
@alphabet = ( a..z ) ;
```

Arrays can have more than one index – to represent multiple dimensions, rather than the single dimension of a regular array. Multi-dimensional arrays of three indices and more are uncommon, but two-dimensional arrays are useful to store grid-based information, such as coordinates – for example:

```
@coords = ( [ 1, 2, 3 ] , [ 4, 5, 6 ] ) ;
```

A two-dimensional array in Perl is essentially an array of arrays, where each dimension contains a comma-separated list of element values within square brackets. An individual element can be referenced using the array name prefixed by a **$** character and followed by a pair of square brackets containing the element number for each dimension. This means that **$coords[0][0]** in the example above references the first element in the first dimension (1) and **$coords[1][0]** references the first element in the second dimension (4).

Don't forget

Array numbering starts at 0 – so the final element in an array of six elements is number 5, not number 6.

	[0]	[1]	[2]
[0]	1	2	3
[1]	4	5	6

...cont'd

The size of an array can be revealed by its scalar context, simply by assigning the array variable to a scalar variable. Additionally, the index of the final element can be discovered using a special $# prefix to the array name.

1 Open a plain text editor and create an array variable containing strings and numbers
```
@arr = ('Alpha', 'Beta', 'Charlie', 4, 8) ;
```

2 Next, output all elements, then selected element values
```
print "\nArray: @arr \n" ;
print "Element 0:\t @arr[0] \n" ;
print "Elements 2 & 4:\t @arr[2,4] \n" ;
```

3 Now, assign ranges to the array, then output all modified array element values and a selected slice of elements
```
@arr = (1..12) ;
print "\nDozen: @arr \n" ;
@arr = (a..z) ;
print "Alphabet: @arr \n" ;
print "Slice: @arr[0..2] \n" ;
```

4 Finally, assign the array to a scalar variable, then output the array size and the index of its final element
```
$arr_size = @arr ;
print "Size: $arr_size \n" ;
print "Final Index: $#arr \n" ;
```

5 Save the file in your scripts folder, named as "array.pl", then, at a Terminal prompt, execute the program
perl array.pl

array.pl

Hot tip

Notice how the range operator can be used to assign and also retrieve a range of array values.

19

```
C:\Scripts>perl array.pl

Array: Alpha Beta Charlie 4 8
Element 0:        Alpha
Elements 2 & 4:   Charlie 8

Dozen: 1 2 3 4 5 6 7 8 9 10 11 12
Alphabet: a b c d e f g h i j k l m n o p q r s t u v w x y z
Slice: a b c

Size: 26
Final Index: 25
```

Manipulating elements

Just as Perl provides the built-in **print** function, Perl provides several built-in functions for the manipulation of array elements:

Function	
push	Adds one or more elements to the end of array.
	push @*array_name*, *value/s* ;
pop	Removes and returns the last element of array.
	$*last_element* = pop @*array_name* ;
shift	Removes and returns the first element of array.
	$*first_element* = shift @*array_name* ;
unshift	Adds one or more elements to the start of array and returns the modified array size.
	$*size* = unshift @*array_name*, *value/s* ;
sort	Returns the elements in alphanumeric order.
	@*array_name* = sort @*array_name* ;
splice	Replaces one or more elements and returns the removed elements.
	@*cut* = splice @*array_name*, *offset*, *length*, *value/s* ;

element.pl

1 Open a plain text editor, then create an array variable containing three string characters and output all elements
`@arr = ('D', 'F', 'B') ;`
`print "\nArray:\t\t @arr \n" ;`

2 Next, add three more characters to the end of the array, then output all six elements
`push @arr , ('E', 'G', 'C') ;`
`print "Pushed:\t\t @arr \n" ;`

3 Now, arrange the array elements into their values' ascending alphanumeric order and output all six elements in their new order
`@arr = sort @arr ;`
`print "Sorted:\t\t @arr \n" ;`

...cont'd

4 Add two more characters to the beginning of the array, then output all elements and the new array size
```
$size = unshift @arr, (100 , 'A' ) ;
print "Unshifted:\t @arr " ;
print "\tSize Now: $size \n" ;
```

5 Next, remove the first element, then output the remaining elements and the value of the removed element
```
$off = shift @arr ;
print "Shifted:\t @arr " ;
print "\t\tRemoved: $off \n" ;
```

6 Now, remove the last element, then output the remaining elements and the value of the removed element
```
$off = pop @arr ;
print "Popped:\t\t @arr " ;
print "\t\tRemoved: $off \n" ;
```

7 Finally, remove three elements (starting at index 3) and replace them in place with three new elements – then output all elements in the modified array and the value of the removed elements
```
@cut = splice @arr, 3, 3 , (1, 2, 3) ;
print "Spliced:\t @arr " ;
print "\t\tReplaced: @cut \n" ;
```

8 Save the file in your scripts folder, named as "element.pl", then, at a Terminal prompt, execute the program to see how the functions have manipulated the array elements
perl element.pl

Hot tip

By default, the **sort** function sorts string values in ascending order according to their numerical ASCII code value – in which A-Z is 65-90 and a-z is 97-122.

Hot tip

When assigning multiple values with a function it is useful, but not essential, to group the list of values within parentheses for clarity.

```
C:\Scripts>perl element.pl

Array:          D F B
Pushed:         D F B E G C
Sorted:         B C D E F G
Unshifted:      100 A B C D E F G    Size Now: 8
Shifted:        A B C D E F G        Removed: 100
Popped:         A B C D E F         Removed: G
Spliced:        A B C 1 2 3          Replaced: D E F

C:\Scripts>
```

21

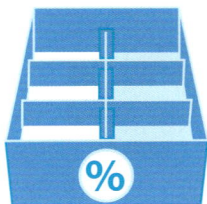

Associating keys

A "hash" is a variable that can store multiple items of data as a series of key-value pairs. A hash variable is declared in the same way as a scalar variable, but a hash name is prefixed by a **%** symbol. Values can be assigned to the hash as a comma-separated list of key-value pairs within parentheses, like this:

```
%hash_name = ( key1 , value1 , key2 , value2 ) ;
```

Alternatively, the key-value pairs can be associated using a **=>** "fat comma" pair constructor operator for better readability, like this:

```
%hash_name = ( key1 => value1, key2 => value2 ) ;
```

The fat comma improves readability and acts as a synonym for the associating comma. Importantly, it also has the advantage of automatically quoting valid "bare words" on the left-hand side.

Any hash pair can be referenced using the syntax of a **$** character followed by the hash name and a key name within **{ }** braces:

```
$hash_name{ key_name }
```

A new pair can be added to the hash by specifying a new key name and assigning an associated value. Conversely, a pair can be removed from the hash using the built-in Perl **delete** function followed by the hash pair reference. Additionally, you can test for the existence of a particular pair using **if exists** Perl keywords (or absence with **if not exists** keywords) and the hash pair reference.

The Perl built-in **foreach** function can iterate over each pair within a hash by retrieving a list of all keys using a built-in **keys** function to assign, in turn, each key to variable. Each key and its associated value can then be output using this syntax:

```
foreach $key_name ( keys %hash_name ) {
    print $key_name = $hash_name{ $key_name } ;
}
```

There is an important gotcha to be aware of here though – the key-value pairs are not certain to be returned in the same order each time, because Perl hashes are <u>unordered</u> data structures. You can, however, use the built-in **sort** function to overcome this:

```
foreach $key_name ( sort keys %hash_name ) {
    print $key_name = $hash_name{ $key_name } ;
}
```

There is also a built-in **values** function that can be used to return a list of all values in a hash.

Notice how functions that do more than simply return a result can contain statements within a "block" enclosed in **{ }** braces.

1 Open a plain text editor, then create a hash variable containing three key-value pairs
```
%ages = ( Bert => 21, Anna => 25, Dave => 28 ) ;
```

hash.pl

2 Next, output all initial keys and values, in unsorted order
```
foreach $key ( keys %ages ) {
    print "$key is $ages{$key}   " ;
}
```

3 Output the value associated with a single key
```
print "\nAnna's age is $ages{Anna} \n" ;
```

4 Now, remove one key-value pair, then add one new pair
```
delete $ages{Dave} ;
$ages{Cleo} = 27 ;
```

5 Then, output all current keys and values, sorted into order
```
foreach $key ( sort keys %ages ) {
    print "$key is $ages{$key}   " ;
}
```

23

6 Finally, report the pairs that have changed
```
print "\nCleo added." if exists $ages{Bert} ;
print "\tDave erased.\n" if not exists $ages{Dave} ;
```

7 Save the file in your scripts folder, named as "hash.pl", then, at a Terminal prompt, execute the program
```
perl hash.pl
```

Don't forget

Repeatedly execute this program to see the unsorted output differ.

```
Command Prompt   ×    +  ⌄               —  □  ×

C:\Scripts>perl hash.pl
Bert is 21    Anna is 25    Dave is 28  ◄
Anna's age is 25
Anna is 25    Bert is 21    Cleo is 27
Cleo added.    Dave erased.

C:\Scripts>
```

```
Command Prompt   ×    +  ⌄               —  □  ×

C:\Scripts>perl hash.pl
Dave is 28    Anna is 25    Bert is 21
Anna's age is 25
Anna is 25    Bert is 21    Cleo is 27
Cleo added.    Dave erased.

C:\Scripts>_
```

Imposing restrictions

With all but the most trivial Perl programs it is recommended to include a **use strict** "pragma" at the beginning of the code to catch potential errors during compilation. This demands that variables must be declared with a "scope modifier" to determine their visibility to various parts of the program. The three keywords most used as scope modifiers are:

- **my** – restricts visibility to the file, block, or subroutine, and is used for private variables.

- **our** – allows visibility across an entire package and is used for global variables.

- **local** – temporarily overrides the value of a global variable but does not create a new variable.

The use of strict mode prevents the use of undeclared variables, makes code easier to debug, and enforces good coding practice. Declaration of a private variable in strict mode looks like this:

```
use strict ;
my $variable_name ;
```

If a variable is declared in strict mode without a scope modifier, the interpreter will report an error and compilation will halt.

Where a private variable is declared inside a block, the interpreter will report an error and compilation will halt if access to that variable is attempted from outside that block.

Conversely, a global variable declared inside a block is accessible from outside that block, so compilation will succeed.

In addition to the recommendation to use strict mode, there is a further recommendation to include a **use warnings** pragma at the beginning of the code to help catch potential errors during execution of the program. These are errors that are not apparent during compilation but that may arise when the program runs.

The use of warnings identifies ambiguous code, alerts you to deprecated features, and encourages good coding practice.

...cont'd

1 Begin a program with use pragmas and a regular variable declaration, then run the program to see compilation fail

```
use strict ;
use warnings ;
$num = 7 ;
```

strict.pl

```
Command Prompt

C:\Scripts>perl strict.pl
Global symbol "$num" requires explicit package name
(did you forget to declare "my $num"?) at strict.pl line 3.
Execution of strict.pl aborted due to compilation errors.
```

2 Add a scope modifier to correct the compilation error and a statement to query the variable value, then run the program to see compilation succeed – but with a warning

```
my $num = 7 ;
if ( $num = 5 ) {
    print "Number is five.\n" ;
}
```

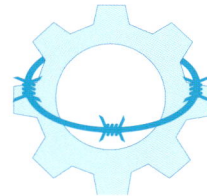

```
Command Prompt

C:\Scripts>perl strict.pl
Found = in conditional, should be == at strict.pl line 5.
Number is five.
```

3 Amend the query to correct the warning error, and add statements to output global and local variable values

```
if ( $num == 5 ) {
    print "Number is five.\n" ;
}

our $name = 'Mike' ;
{
    local $name = 'Jane' ;
    print "Temporary Name: $name \n" ;
}
print "Global Name: $name \n" ;
```

```
Command Prompt

C:\Scripts>perl strict.pl
Temporary Name: Jane
Global Name: Mike
```

Beware

Subsequent examples in this book will each begin with the **use strict** pragma and **use warnings** pragma.

Summary

- Perl is known as the Swiss Army Knife of programming languages and as "the duct tape of the Internet".

- The Comprehensive Perl Archive Network (CPAN) provides access to over 25,000 Perl modules.

- Linux and macOS operating systems have Perl installed by default, but Perl must be manually installed on Windows.

- Each Perl script file must be given a name of your choice followed by a **.pl** or **.PL** file extension.

- Literal text strings can be enclosed in single quotes but double quotes must be used to allow interpolation.

- Perl variables store data values in computer memory.

- A scalar variable stores a single data value of any data type.

- An array variable stores multiple data values sequentially in array elements that can be referenced by a zero-based index.

- Values are assigned to array elements as a comma-separated list within parentheses.

- The range operator is a shortcut that can assign sequential numbers and letters to an array variable.

- A two-dimensional array assigns each dimension as a comma-separated list of element values within square brackets.

- Perl provides several built-in functions for the manipulation of array elements.

- A hash variable stores multiple items of data as a series of key-value pairs.

- Perl hashes are unordered data structures, so key-value pairs are not certain to be returned in the same order each time.

- Strict mode demands that variables must be declared with a scope modifier to determine their visibility.

- Strict mode identifies compilation errors, and warnings identify ambiguous code during execution of a program.

2 Performing Operations

This chapter introduces the Perl operators and demonstrates the operations they can perform.

Doing arithmetic

The arithmetical operators commonly used in Perl programs are listed in the table below, together with the operation they perform:

Operator	Operation
+	Addition
-	Subtraction
*	Multiplication
/	Division
%	Modulus (Remainder)
**	Exponentiation
++	Increment
--	Decrement

The operators for addition, subtraction, multiplication, and division act as you would expect. Expressions containing more than one operator can be bracketed for clarity – operations within innermost parentheses are performed first:

```
$a = $b * $c - $d % $e / $f ;      // This is unclear.

$a = ( $b * $c ) - ( ( $d % $e ) / $f ) ;      // This is clearer.
```

The % modulus operator will divide the first given number by the second given number and return the remainder of the operation.

The ** exponentiation operator will raise the first number to the power of the second.

The ++ increment operator and -- decrement operator alter the given number by 1 and return the resulting value. The increment and decrement operators can, however, be placed before or after a value to different effect. If placed before the operand (prefix) its value is immediately changed, but if placed after the operand (postfix) its value is noted first, then the value is changed.

Hot tip

Values used with operators to form expressions are called "operands" – in the expression 2 + 3 the numerical values 2 and 3 are the operands.

...cont'd

Perl allows you to interpolate expressions within strings using this special syntax:

@{ [*expression*] }

The special syntax is used in the script below to output the result of each arithmetic operation.

1 Begin a Perl program by declaring two scalar variables
```perl
use strict ;
use warnings ;
my $a = 8 ;
my $b = 4 ;
```

arithmetic.pl

2 Next, add statements to output the result of each basic arithmetic operation
```perl
print "\nAddition:\t @{[$a + $b]} \n" ;
print "Subtract:\t @{[$a - $b]} \n" ;
print "Multiply:\t @{[$a * $b]} \n" ;
print "Division:\t @{[$a / $b]} \n" ;
print "Exponent:\t @{[$a ** $b]} \n" ;
```

3 Now, insert statements to output the result of both postfix and prefix increment operations – to see how they differ
```perl
print "Postfix increment: @{[$a++]} " ;
print "\tPostfix result: $a \n" ;
print "Prefix increment:  @{[++$b]} " ;
print "\tPrefix result:  $b \n" ;
```

A prefix operator changes the variable value immediately – a postfix operator changes the value subsequently.

4 Save the file in your scripts folder, named as "arithmetic.pl", then run this arithmetic program
```
perl arithmetic.pl
```

```
C:\Scripts>perl arithmetic.pl

Addition:       12
Subtract:       4
Multiply:       32
Division:       2
Exponent:       4096
Postfix increment: 8      Postfix result: 9
Prefix increment:  5      Prefix result:  5
```

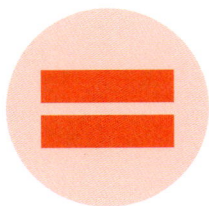

Assigning values

The operators that are used in Perl programming to assign values are listed in the table below. All except the simple = assignment operator are a shorthand form of a longer equivalent expression:

Operator	Example	Equivalent
=	$a = $b	$a = $b
+=	$a += $b	$a = ($a + $b)
-=	$a -= $b	$a = ($a - $b)
*=	$a *= $b	$a = ($a * $b)
/=	$a /= $b	$a = ($a / $b)
**=	$a **= $b	$a = ($a ** $b)
%=	$a %= $b	$a = ($a % $b)

In the first example above, variable **$a** is assigned the value that is contained in variable **$b** – so that becomes the new value stored in the **a** variable.

The **+=** operator is useful to add a value onto an existing value that is stored in the **$a** variable.

In the table example, the **+=** operator first adds the value contained in variable **$a** to the value contained in variable **$b**. It then assigns the result to become the new value in variable **$a**.

All the other operators work in the same way by making the arithmetical operation between the two values first, then assigning the result of that operation to the first variable – to become its new stored value.

With the **%=** operator, the first operand **$a** is divided by the second operand **$b**, then the remainder of that operation is assigned to variable **$a**.

In Perl you can declare multiple variables without assigning values to initialize the variables by specifying them as a comma-separated list within parentheses.

Don't forget

It is important to regard the = operator to mean "assign" rather than "equals" to avoid confusion with the == equality operator.

...cont'd

1 Begin a Perl program by declaring two scalar variables without initial values

```perl
use strict ;
use warnings ;
my ($a, $b) ;
```

assign.pl

2 Next, use the simple assignment operator to initialize the variables, then output their values

```perl
$a = 8 ;
$b = 4 ;
print "\na = $a\tb = $b\n" ;
```

3 Now, add statements to output combined assigned values

```perl
print "Add & assign:\t\t" ;
print "a += b (8 += 4 )\ta = @{[$a += $b]} \n" ;

print "Subtract & assign:\t" ;
print "a -= b (12 -= 4 )\ta = @{[$a -= $b]} \n" ;

print "Multiply & assign:\t" ;
print "a *= b (8 *= 4 )\ta = @{[$a *= $b]} \n" ;

print "Divide & assign:\t" ;
print "a /= b (32 /= 4 )\ta = @{[$a /= $b]} \n" ;

print "Assign exponent:\t" ;
print "a **= b (8 **= 4 )\ta = @{[$a **= $b]} \n" ;

print "Assign remainder:\t" ;
print "a %= b (8 %= 4 )\ta = @{[$a %= $b]} \n" ;
```

4 Save the file in your scripts folder, named as "assign.pl", then run this assignment program

perl assign.pl

Beware

Unlike the = assign operator, the == equality operator compares operands and is described on page 32.

```
Command Prompt  ×   +  ∨                    —   □   ×

C:\Scripts>perl assign.pl

a = 8   b = 4
Add & assign:          a += b (8 += 4 )      a = 12
Subtract & assign:     a -= b (12 -= 4 )     a = 8
Multiply & assign:     a *= b (8 *= 4 )      a = 32
Divide & assign:       a /= b (32 /= 4 )     a = 8
Assign exponent:       a **= b (8 **= 4)     a = 4096
Assign remainder:      a %= b (8 %= 4 )      a = 0
```

Comparing values

The operators that are commonly used in Perl programming to compare numerical and string values are listed in the table below:

Operator (Numbers)	Operator (Strings)	Comparative Test
==	eq	Equality
!=	ne	Inequality
>	gt	Greater than
<	lt	Less than
>=	ge	Greater than or equal to
<=	le	Less than or equal to
<=>	cmp	Three-way comparison

Hot tip

The **cmp** operator uses the ASCII code values to compare strings. A-Z uppercase characters have ASCII code values 65-90, and a-z lowercase characters have ASCII code values 97-122.

The == and **eq** equality operators compare two operands and evaluate as true (1) if both are equal, otherwise the condition is false. Conversely, the != (≠) and **ne** inequality operators evaluate as true (1) if both are not equal, otherwise the condition is false.

The > and **gt** "greater than" operators compare two operands and evaluate as true (1) if the first is greater in value than the second, otherwise the condition is false. The < and **lt** "less than" operators make the same comparison but evaluate as true (1) if the first operand is less than the second, otherwise the condition is false.

The >= (≥) and **ge** "greater than or equal to" operators also evaluate as true (1) if the two operands are exactly equal in value. Similarly the <= (≤) and **le** "less than or equal to" operators also evaluate as true (1) if the two operands are equal in value.

The <=> "spaceship operator" and **cmp** operator compare two operands and return -1 if the first operand is less than the second operand, or return 0 if the operands are equal, or return 1 if the first operand is greater than the second operand.

In Perl you can declare and initialize multiple variables by assigning a comma-separated list of values within parentheses.

1 Begin a Perl program by declaring four scalar variables with assigned initial values

```perl
use strict ;
use warnings ;
my ($a, $b) = (8, 4) ;
my ($s, $t) = ('Perl', 'perl') ;
```

compare.pl

2 Next, use the comparison operators to compare numerical values and output the result of each comparison

```perl
print "\na > b?\t @{[$a > $b]} \t" ;
print "a == b?\t @{[$a == $b]} \t" ;
print "a < b?\t @{[$a < $b]} \n" ;

print "a >= b?\t @{[$a >= $b]} \t" ;
print "a != b?\t @{[$a != $b]} \t" ;
print "a <=> b? @{[$a <=> $b]} \n\n" ;
```

3 Now, use the comparison operators to compare string values and output the result of each comparison

```perl
print "$s gt $t? @{[$s gt $t]}   " ;
print "$s eq $t? @{[$s eq $t]}   " ;
print "$s lt $t? @{[$s lt $t]} \n" ;

print "$s le $t? @{[$s le $t]}   " ;
print "$s ne $t? @{[$s ne $t]}   " ;
print "$s cmp $t? @{[$s cmp $t]} \n" ;
```

4 Save the file in your scripts folder, named as "compare.pl", then run this comparison program

perl compare.pl

```
Command Prompt    ×    + ∨                              —    □    ×

C:\Scripts>perl compare.pl

a > b?  1       a == b?         a < b?
a ≥ b?  1       a ≠ b? 1        a ⟺ b? 1

Perl gt perl?       Perl eq perl?       Perl lt perl? 1
Perl le perl? 1     Perl ne perl? 1     Perl cmp perl? −1
```

Hot tip

These comparison operators are also known as "relational operators".

Assessing logic

The logical operators most commonly used in Perl programming are listed in the table below:

Operator	Operator	Operation
&&	and	Both perform logical AND
||	or	Both perform logical OR
	xor	Performs logical eXclusive OR
!	not	Both perform logical NOT

The logical operators are used with operands or expressions that can evaluate to Boolean values of true or false.

The logical AND operators will evaluate two operands and the condition will be true (1) if both operands are themselves true, otherwise the condition will be false. This is used in conditional branching where the direction of a program is determined by testing two conditions – if both conditions are satisfied, the program will go in a certain direction, otherwise it will take a different direction.

Unlike the AND operators that need both operands to be true, the OR operators will evaluate their two operands and the condition will be true if either one of the operands is itself true. The XOR operator will return true if only one operand is true.

The logical NOT operators are unary operators that are used before a single operand. They invert the value of the given operand, so if an operand evaluates as true, the NOT operator will set the condition to false. This is useful in Perl programming to toggle the value of a variable in successive loop iterations to ensure that on each pass, the value is inverted – like flicking a light switch on and off.

In Perl programs, a Boolean false value can be represented by the number **0**, the string **'0'**, an empty string **''** (or **""**), the keyword **undef** (an undefined value), or an empty list **()**. Everything else, such as the number **1**, represents the Boolean true value.

34

Beware

Where there is more than one logical operator expression, each expression must be enclosed by parentheses.

The term "Boolean" refers to a system of logical thought developed by the English mathematician George Boole (1815-1864).

1 Begin a Perl program by declaring two scalar variables with assigned initial values
```perl
use strict ;
use warnings ;
my ($a, $b) = (1, 0) ;
```

logic.pl

2 Next, simply output the variable values
```perl
print "\na = $a \tb = $b \n\n" ;
```

3 Now, use the logical AND operators to evaluate the variable Boolean states and output the results
```perl
print "a and a = @{[$a && $a]} \t" ;
print "a and b = @{[$a and $b]} \t" ;
print "b and b = @{[$b && $b]} \n\n" ;
```

4 Then, use the logical OR operators to evaluate the variable Boolean states and output the results
```perl
print "a or a = @{[$a || $a]} \t" ;
print "a or b = @{[$a or $b]} \t" ;
print "b or b = @{[$b or $b]} \n\n" ;
```

5 Finally, use the logical NOT operators to output the inverted variable Boolean states
```perl
print "not a = @{[0 + !$a]} \t" ;
print "not b = @{[0 + not $b]} \n" ;
```

The additions in the NOT expressions are simply used to force a numeric context for the output.

6 Save the file in your scripts folder, named as "logic.pl", then run this logic evaluation program
```
perl logic.pl
```

35

```
Command Prompt    +  ∨                        —  □  ✕

C:\Scripts>perl logic.pl

a = 1    b = 0

a and a = 1     a and b = 0     b and b = 0

a or a = 1      a or b = 1      b or b = 0

not a = 0       not b = 1
```

Examining conditions

Perl provides a useful **?:** "ternary" operator to examine conditions. This operator first evaluates an expression for a true or false condition, then returns one of two specified values depending on the result of the evaluation. For this reason it is also known as the "conditional" operator.

The **?:** ternary operator has this syntax:

> (*test-expression*) **?** *if-true-return-this* **:** *if-false-return-this* ;

Although the ternary operator can initially appear a little confusing, it is well worth becoming familiar with this operator, as it can execute powerful program branching with minimal code – for example, to branch when a variable is not a value of 1:

> (*$variable* != 1) **?** *if-true-do-this* **:** *if-false-do-this* ;

The ternary operator is commonly used in Perl programming to assign the maximum or minimum value of two variables to a third variable – for example, to assign a minimum, like this:

> **$c = ($a < $b) ? $a : $b ;**

The expression in parentheses represents a true condition only when the value of variable **$a** is less than that of variable **$b** – so the lesser value in variable **$a** gets assigned to variable **$c**.

Similarly, replacing the **<** less than operator in the test expression with the **>** greater than operator would assign the greater value of variable **$b** to variable **$c**.

Another common use of the ternary operator incorporates the **%** modulus operator in the test expression to determine whether the value of a variable is an odd number or an even number:

> (*$variable* % 2 != 0) **?** *if-true(odd)-do-this* **:** *if-false(even)-do-this* ;

Where the result of dividing the variable value by two does leave a remainder, the number is odd – where there is no remainder, the number is even.

The test expression (*$variable* % 2 == 1) would have the same effect but it is preferable to test for inequality – it's easier to spot when something is different than when it's identical.

Don't forget

The ternary operator has three operands – the one before the **?**, and those before and after the **:**.

...cont'd

1 Begin a Perl program by declaring two scalar variables with assigned initial values

```perl
use strict ;
use warnings ;
my ($a, $b) = (1, 4) ;
```

ternary.pl

2 Next, simply output the variable values

```perl
print "\na = $a \tb = $b \n\n" ;
```

3 Now, use the ternary operator to evaluate the first variable value and output appropriate results

```perl
print "a is @{[$a != 1 ? 'not one' : 'one']} \t" ;
print "a is @{[$a % 2 != 0 ? 'odd' : 'even']} \n\n" ;
```

4 Then, use the ternary operator to evaluate the second variable value and output appropriate results

```perl
print "b is @{[$b != 1 ? 'not one' : 'one']} \t" ;
print "b is @{[$b % 2 != 0 ? 'odd' : 'even']} \n\n" ;
```

5 Finally, use the ternary operator to evaluate both variable values and output the greater and lesser of the two values

```perl
print "Maximum is @{[$a > $b ? $a : $b]} \n" ;
print "Minimum is @{[$a < $b ? $a : $b]} \n" ;
```

6 Save the file in your scripts folder, named as "ternary.pl", then run this conditional program

```
perl ternary.pl
```

37

Hot tip

Use the ternary operator to write concise conditional expressions and embed conditional testing directly within assignments.

```
Command Prompt    +  v                        —   □   ×

C:\Scripts>perl ternary.pl

a = 1    b = 4

a is one        a is odd

b is not one    b is even

Maximum is 4
Minimum is 1
```

Juggling bits

In computer terms, each byte comprises eight bits that can each contain a **1** or a **0** to store a binary number, representing decimal values from 0 to 255. Each bit contributes a decimal component only when that bit contains a **1**. Components are designated right-to-left from the "Least Significant Bit" (LSB) to the "Most Significant Bit" (MSB). The binary number in the bit pattern below is **00110010** and represents the decimal number 50 (2+16+32):

Bit No.	8 MSB	7	6	5	4	3	2	1 LSB
Decimal	128	64	32	16	8	4	2	1
Binary	0	0	1	1	0	0	1	0

It is possible to manipulate individual bit parts of a byte using the Perl "bitwise" logical operators listed below:

Operator	Name	Example
&	Bitwise AND	0011 & 0101 = 0001
|	Bitwise OR	0011 | 0101 = 0111
^	Bitwise Exclusive XOR	0011 ^ 0101 = 0110
~	Bitwise NOT	~ 0101 = 1010

Hot tip

Each half of a byte is known as a "nibble" (four bits). The binary numbers in the examples in the table describe values stored in a nibble.

The **&** AND operator compares each bit of two integers and sets a bit to 1 if that bit value in each integer is also 1, otherwise the bit is set to 0.

```
0011
0101
0001
```

The **|** OR operator compares each bit of two integers and sets a bit to 1 if that bit value in either integer is also 1, otherwise the bit is set to 0.

```
0011
0101
0111
```

The **^** Exclusive XOR operator compares each bit of two integers and sets a bit to 1 if the bits differ, otherwise the bit is set to 0.

```
0011
0101
0110
```

The **~** NOT operator simply reverses each bit value.

```
0101
1010
```

In addition to the bitwise logical operators, Perl also provides these bitwise shift operators that can move bits left or right:

Operator	Name	Example
<<	Left Shift	0010 << 2 = 1000
>>	Right Shift	1000 >> 2 = 0010

Bitwise operations can be used to easily swap the values between two variables. To see this in action, the built-in Perl **printf** (print formatted) function can be used to format numerical values for output as binary nibbles using a **%.4b** placeholder.

1 Begin a Perl program by declaring two scalar variables with assigned initial values
```perl
use strict ;
use warnings ;
my ($a, $b) = (4, 8) ;
```

2 Next, output both variable values in decimal and binary
```perl
printf("\na:\t $a \t%.4b\nb:\t $b \t%.4b\n", $a, $b ) ;
```

3 Now, manipulate the bits to exchange the variable values
```perl
$a = $a ^ $b ;  $b = $a ^ $b ;  $a = $a ^ $b ;
```

4 Output the variable values in decimal and binary again
```perl
printf("\na:\t $a \t%.4b\nb:\t $b \t%.4b\n", $a, $b ) ;
```

5 Save the file in your scripts folder, named as "bitwise.pl", then run this bitwise program
```
perl bitwise.pl
```

PL

bitwise.pl

39

Hot tip

Other placeholders that can be used with the **printf** function include...
%d (decimal)
%x (hexadecimal)
%o (octal)
%s (string)

```
Command Prompt    +  ∨                    □   ✕

C:\Scripts>perl bitwise.pl

a:      4       0100
b:      8       1000

a:      8       1000
b:      4       0100
```

Respecting precedence

Operator precedence determines the order in which Perl evaluates expressions. For example, in the expression **a = 6 + 8 * 3**, the order of precedence determines that multiplication is completed first.

Expressions containing multiple operators of equal precedence is determined by "operator associativity" – grouping operands with the one on the left (LTR) or on the right (RTL). The table below lists operator precedence in descending order – those on the top row have highest precedence. Operators with the same level of precedence are grouped together:

Don't forget

The * multiply operator is on a higher row than the + addition operator – so in the expression **a=6+8*3**, multiplication is completed first, before the addition, so **a = 6 + 24 (30)** not **a = 14 * 3 (42)**.

40

Operator	Operation	Direction
->	Dereference	LTR
++ --	Increment and Decrement	None
**	Exponentiation	RTL
! ~ + -	Symbolic unary	RTL
* / % x	Multiplicative	LTR
+ - .	Additive	LTR
<< >>	Shift	LTR
< > <= >= lt gt le ge	Comparison	None
== != <=> eq ne cmp	Equality	None
&	Bitwise AND	LTR
| ^	Bitwise OR and XOR	LTR
&&	Logical AND	LTR
|| //	Logical OR and Defined-OR	LTR
.. ...	Range and Yada Yada	None
?:	Ternary conditional	LTR
= += -= *= /= **=	Assignment	RTL
, =>	Comma	LTR
not	Logical NOT	RTL
and	Logical AND	LTR
or xor	Logical OR and XOR	LTR

1 Begin a Perl program that declares one scalar variable
```perl
use strict ;
use warnings ;
my $number ;
```

order.pl

2 Next, add statements that evaluate an expression and output the result
```perl
$number = 1 + 4 * 3 ;
print "\nDefault order:\t $number \n" ;
```

3 Now, add parentheses to edit the expression, then output the modified result
```perl
$number = (1 + 4) * 3 ;
print "\nForced order:\t $number \n" ;
```

4 Then, add statements to evaluate a new expression and output the result
```perl
$number = 7 - 4 + 2 ;
print "\nDefault direction:\t $number \n" ;
```

5 Finally, add parentheses to edit the new expression, then output the modified result and end the program
```perl
$number = 7 - (4 + 2) ;
print "\nForced direction:\t $number\n" ;
```

6 Save the file in your scripts folder, named as "order.pl", then run this precedence program
```
perl order.pl
```

```
Command Prompt    X    +  ⌄                        —    □    ✕

C:\Scripts>perl order.pl

Default order:   13

Forced order:    15

Default direction:      5

Forced direction:       1
```

Summary

- Arithmetical operators can form expressions with two operands for addition **+**, subtraction **-**, multiplication *****, or division **/**.

- The **%** modulus operator divides the first given operand by the second operand and returns the remainder of the operation.

- The ****** exponentiation operator raises the first operand to the power of the second operand.

- Increment **++** and decrement **--** operators modify a single operand by a value of 1.

- When the increment **++** or decrement **--** operators prefix an operand its value is immediately changed, but if they postfix an operand its value is noted first, then the value is changed.

- The assignment **=** operator can be combined with an arithmetical operator to perform an arithmetical calculation, then assign its result.

- Comparison operators can form expressions comparing two numeric operands for equality **==**, inequality **!=**, greater **>**, lesser **<**, greater or equal **>=**, and lesser or equal **<=** values.

- Comparison operators can form expressions comparing two string operands for equality **eq**, inequality **ne**, greater **gt**, lesser **lt**, greater or equal **ge**, and lesser or equal **le** values.

- Logical **and** (**&&**), **or** (**||**) and **xor** operators can be used to evaluate two operands for a Boolean condition of true or false.

- The logical **not** (**!**) operator returns the inverse Boolean value of a single operand.

- A ternary **?:** operator evaluates a given Boolean expression, then returns one of two operands depending on its result.

- Bitwise **&** AND, **|** OR, **^** XOR, and **~** NOT operators can be used to manipulate individual bit parts of a byte.

- Operator precedence determines the order in which Perl evaluates expressions.

- It is important to explicitly set operator precedence in complex expressions by adding parentheses **( )**.

3 Controlling Flow

This chapter demonstrates Perl conditional statements, which allow programs to branch in different directions, and Perl repeating loop structures.

Branching if

The Perl **if** keyword performs the basic conditional test that evaluates a given expression for a Boolean value of true or false. The conditional test must be enclosed within **( )** parentheses.

Statements to be executed when the expression is found to be true form the body of a code block. The conditional test is followed by one space and an **{** opening brace. The statements inside the code block should each be indented by four spaces and the code block should end with a **}** closing brace without indentation. The syntax of the **if** statement block therefore looks like this:

```
if ( condition ) {
    statement/s-to-execute-when-condition-is-true
}
```

Hot tip
Shorthand can be used when testing a Boolean value – so the expression **if (flag == .true.)** can be written as **if (flag)**.

Optionally, an **if** statement can offer alternative statements to execute when the test fails by appending an **else** statement block after the **if** statement block, like this:

```
if ( condition ) {
    statements-to-execute-when-condition-is-true
}
else {
    statements-to-execute-when-condition-is-false
}
```

This operation performs "conditional branching", which allows the program to proceed in different directions according to the result of the conditional test. It can be represented visually by a flowchart:

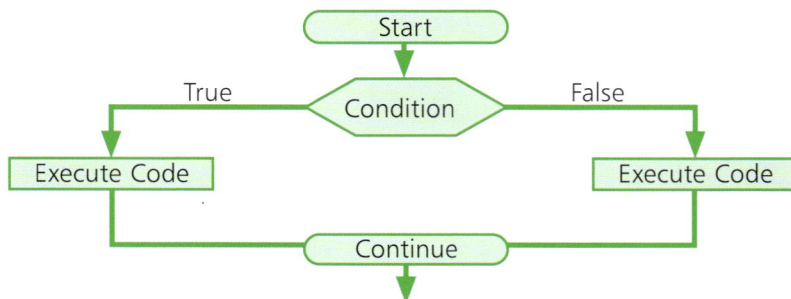

Hot tip
You may see the **else** "cuddled" by placing it on the same line as the closing brace of the **if** code block as
} else {
but this is not recommended.

Short **if** statements can be written on a single line, like this:

```
statement-to-execute-when-condition-is-true if ( condition )
```

...cont'd

1 Begin a Perl program by declaring a scalar variable
```perl
use strict ;
use warnings ;
my $angle ;
```

PL

ifelse.pl

2 Next, initialize the variable with a floating-point value
```perl
$angle = 90.0 ;
```

3 Now, add a conditional test for equality
```perl
if ( $angle == 90.0 ) {
    print "\nAngle: $angle degrees\n" ;
    print "Corner is a right angle.\n" ;
}
```

4 Then, increase the value within the variable
```perl
$angle += 15 ;
```

5 Finally, add conditional tests for comparison
```perl
if ( $angle < 90.0 ) {
    print "\nAngle: $angle degrees\n" ;
    print "Corner is acute.\n" ;
}
else {
    print "\nAngle: $angle degrees\n" ;
    print "Corner is obtuse.\n" ;
}
```

Beware

Don't leave additional whitespace or line breaks between the closing brace of the **if** code block and the **else** keyword.

6 Save the file in your scripts folder, named as "ifelse.pl", then run this branching program
```
perl ifelse.pl
```

```
Command Prompt       X     +  v                    —    □   ✕

C:\Scripts>perl ifelse.pl

Angle: 90 degrees
Corner is a right angle.

Angle: 105 degrees
Corner is obtuse.
```

Adding branches

The **if else** conditional test, introduced on page 45, can be extended to evaluate a series of conditions by inserting one or more **elsif** code blocks. When a condition is found to be true, the statements in the associated code block will be executed and no following conditions will be evaluated. The syntax looks like this:

```
if ( condition_1 ) {
        statement/s-to-execute-when-condition_1-is-true
}
elsif ( condition_2 ) {
        statement/s-to-execute-when-condition_2-is-true
}
elsif ( condition_3 ) {
        statement/s-to-execute-when-condition_3-is-true
}
else {
        statement/s-to-execute-when-no-conditions-are-true
}
```

Hot tip

Optionally, you may omit the final **else** code block.

As an alternative to the **if** keyword, which tests for a true condition, Perl also provides an **unless** keyword, which performs a conditional test for false – the opposite of the **if** test:

```
unless ( condition ) {
        statement/s-to-execute-when-condition-is-false
}
```

The **unless** conditional test can also be combined with **else** and extended by inserting **elsif** code blocks, with this syntax:

```
unless ( condition_1 ) {
        statement/s-to-execute-when-condition_1-is-false
}
elsif ( condition_2 ) {
        statement/s-to-execute-when-condition_2-is-true
}
elsif ( condition_3 ) {
        statement/s-to-execute-when-condition_3-is-true
}
else {
        statement/s-to-execute-when-no-conditions-are-true
}
```

Beware

Combining **unless** with **elsif** and **else** can impair readability of the code. It is better to use only **if**, **elsif**, and **else** to make conditional tests.

1 Begin a Perl program by declaring an initialized variable
```perl
use strict ;
use warnings ;
my $age = 24 ;
```

PL

elsif.pl

2 Next, add a series of conditional **if** tests to evaluate the variable value
```perl
if ( $age < 13 ) {
    print "\nAt $age: you are a minor.\n" ;
}
elsif ( $age < 20 ) {
    print "\nAt $age: you are a teenager.\n" ;
}
elsif ( $age < 65 ) {
    print "\nAt $age: you are an adult.\n" ;
}
else {
    print "\nAt $age: you are a senior.\n" ;
}
```

3 Now, add an **unless** test to evaluate the variable value
```perl
unless ( $age > 20 ) {
    print "You have the spirit of youth.\n" ;
}
else {
    print "Like fine wine, you are mature.\n" ;
}
```

4 Save the file in your scripts folder, named as "elsif.pl", then run this program and change the variable value to see that appropriate messages are output
perl elsif.pl

```
Command Prompt ✕      +  ✕                    —   ☐   ✕

C:\Scripts>perl elsif.pl

At 14: you are a teenager.
You have the spirit of youth.

C:\Scripts>perl elsif.pl

At 24: you are an adult.
Like fine wine, you are mature.
```

47

Looping for

A loop is a piece of code in a program that automatically repeats. One complete execution of all statements contained within the loop block is known as an "iteration" or a "pass".

The number of iterations made by a loop is controlled by a conditional test made within the loop. While the tested expression remains true, the loop will continue until the tested expression becomes false – at which time the loop will end.

The three types of loop structures in Perl programming are **for** loops, **while** loops, and **do** loops. Perhaps the most commonly used loop is the **for** loop, which has this syntax:

```
for ( initializer ; condition ; incrementer/decrementer ) {
    statement/s-to-execute-if-condition-is-true
}
```

The **for** loop initializer sets the starting value for a counter of the number of iterations made by the loop. A variable is used for this purpose and is traditionally named "i" (for "index").

Upon each iteration of the **for** loop, the condition is evaluated, and that iteration will only continue while this expression is true. When the condition becomes false, the loop ends immediately without executing the statements again. On each iteration, the counter is incremented and the statements are executed.

Loops may be nested within other loops – so that the inner loop will fully execute its iterations on each iteration of the outer loop.

PL

forloop.pl

① Begin a Perl program by declaring an initialized variable array and a scalar variable recording the array length
```perl
use strict ;
use warnings ;
my @arr = (1, 2, 3) ;
my $len = scalar @arr ;
```

② Next, add a loop to output all array element values
```perl
for ( my $i = 0 ; $i < $len ; $i++ ) {
    print "\nOuter loop iteration: $arr[$i] \n" ;

    // Inner loop to be inserted here (Step 4).
}
```

...cont'd

3 Save the file in your scripts folder, named as "forloop.pl", then run this program to see the loop output
perl forloop.pl

```
Command Prompt   ×   +  ∨                          –   □   ×

C:\Scripts>perl forloop.pl

Outer loop iteration: 1

Outer loop iteration: 2

Outer loop iteration: 3
```

4 Now, insert a nested loop to output each array element value upon each iteration of the outer loop

```
for ( my $j = 0 ; $j < $len ; $j++ ) {
    print "\t\Inner loop iteration: $arr[$j] \n" ;
}
```

5 Save the file once more, then run this program again to see the loop output and the nested loop output
perl forloop.pl

```
Command Prompt   ×   +  ∨                          –   □   ×

C:\Scripts>perl forloop.pl

Outer loop iteration: 1
                Inner loop iteration: 1
                Inner loop iteration: 2
                Inner loop iteration: 3

Outer loop iteration: 2
                Inner loop iteration: 1
                Inner loop iteration: 2
                Inner loop iteration: 3

Outer loop iteration: 3
                Inner loop iteration: 1
                Inner loop iteration: 2
                Inner loop iteration: 3
```

Hot tip

Arrays normally exist in a "list context", returning their elements as a list, but when an array is evaluated in a scalar context (using the **scalar** keyword), they return the length of the array.

49

Looping while

An alternative to the **for** loop, introduced on page 49, uses the **while** keyword, followed by a condition to be evaluated. While the condition remains true, statements in the loop block will be executed until the condition is found to be false.

The loop <u>must</u> contain code that will affect the condition in order to change the evaluation result to false, otherwise an infinite loop is created that will lock the system! Typically, this will change the value of a counter variable that is declared before the loop and included in the tested condition, with this syntax:

```
initializer
while ( condition ) {
    statement/s-to-execute-if-condition-is-true
    incrementer/decrementer
}
```

Optionally, the statement to change the condition can be located in a final **continue** block that will run after each loop iteration:

```
initializer
while ( condition ) {
    statement/s-to-execute-if-condition-is-true
}
continue {
    incrementer/decrementer
}
```

A subtle variation of the **while** loop places the **do** keyword before the loop's statement block, and a **while** test after it, with this syntax:

```
initializer
do {
    statement/s-to-execute-if-condition-is-true
    incrementer/decrementer
} while ( condition )
```

There is also an **until** loop that will continue executing its statements until its test condition becomes true – a reverse alternative to the **while** and **do while** loops:

```
initializer
until ( condition ) {
    statement/s-to-execute-if-condition-is-false
    incrementer/decrementer
}
```

Hot tip

If you accidentally start running an infinite loop, press the **Ctrl + C** keys to terminate the process.

Hot tip

Unlike a **while** loop, which may never execute its statements if the condition is initially false, a **do while** loop will always execute its statements at least once – because the condition is not evaluated until after the first iteration of the loop.

...cont'd

1 Begin a Perl program with two initialized variables
```perl
use strict ;
use warnings ;
my ( $count, $input ) = ( 5, " ) ;
```

2 Next, add a **while** loop to make five iterations, then output a final message
```perl
while ( $count > 0 ) {
    print "\n $count" ;
    $count-- ;
}

print "Blast Off! \n\n" ;
```

3 Now, add a **do while** loop to continue iterations until it receives specified user input
```perl
do {
    print 'Continue? Y/N : ' ;
    $input = <STDIN> ;
    chomp $input ;
} while ( uc $input ne 'N' ) ;

print "Program Ends. \n" ;
```

4 Save the file in your scripts folder, named as "while.pl", then run this program to see the loop output
perl while.pl

```
Command Prompt          ×      +   ∨           —    □    ×

C:\Scripts>perl while.pl

5
4
3
2
1
Blast Off!

Continue? Y/N : y
Continue? Y/N : no
Continue? Y/N : n
Program Ends.
```

PL

while.pl

Hot tip

Here, **<STDIN>** is used to read Standard Input from the keyboard. The built-in **chomp** function removes the trailing newline from the input, and the built-in **uc** function converts lowercase character input to uppercase for the comparison.

Looping each

The terms "array" and "list" are often seen as interchangeable in Perl, but there is a distinct difference between them. An array is a variable whose scalar values are stored in elements and can be manipulated later, whereas a list is a temporary structure whose collection of scalar values are used directly in an expression.

Perl provides a **foreach** keyword that is used to iterate over all values in an array, or all values in a list. The **foreach** keyword assigns the current value in turn to a scalar variable as it iterates across all the values. The current value is automatically assigned to a special **$_** default variable, or you can specify your own variable after the **foreach** keyword. This is followed by parentheses, specifying the array or list, then a code block containing statements to execute on each iteration. The syntax looks like this:

```
foreach variable ( array/list ) {
    statement/s-to-execute-until-there-are-no-more-values
}
```

A **foreach** loop to iterate across array elements using the default special **$_** variable for concision might look like this:

```
foreach ( @array ) {
    print $_ ;
}
```

A **foreach** loop can also iterate across all keys and values in a hash by using a built-in **keys** function to first retrieve all the keys from the hash. Each key can then be used in turn to reference its associated value, with this syntax:

```
foreach variable ( keys %hash ) {
    statement/s-to-execute-until-there-are-no-more-keys
}
```

A **foreach** loop to iterate across hash keys and values using the default special **$_** variable for concision might look like this:

```
foreach ( keys %hash ) {
    print $_  => $hash{ $_ } ;
}
```

Hot tip

In Perl, the keywords **for** and **foreach** are actually interchangeable as they serve the same purpose. The preference in this book is to use **for** when the loop structure uses a counter, and **foreach** when the loop automatically iterates across all values, as shown here.

1   Begin a Perl program by declaring scalar variables and initialized array and hash variables

```perl
use strict ;
use warnings ;
my ( $element, $item, $key ) ;
my @arr = ( 'A', 'B', 'C' ) ;
my %ages = ( Bert => 21, Anna => 25, Cleo => 27 ) ;
```

foreach.pl

2   Next, add a **foreach** loop to output a description followed by all element values in the array variable

```perl
print "\nArray Elements: " ;

foreach $element ( @arr ) {
    print "\t $element \t" ;
}
```

3   Now, add a **foreach** loop to output a description followed by all values in a list

```perl
print "\n\nList Items:\t" ;

foreach $item ( 1..3 ) {
    print "\t $item \t" ;
}
```

4   Then, add a **foreach** loop to output a description followed by all sorted keys and values in a hash variable

```perl
print "\n\nHash Keys & Values:" ;

foreach $key ( sort keys %ages ) {
    print "\t $key: $ages{$key}   " ;
}
```

Don't forget

A hash is an unordered structure, so the key-value pairs may be retrieved in any order – unless the **sort** function is used to order them.

5   Save the file in your scripts folder, named as "foreach.pl", then run this program to see the loop output

perl foreach.pl

```
Command Prompt   ×   +  ∨                          —   □   ×

C:\Scripts>perl foreach.pl

Array Elements:          A              B              C

List Items:              1              2              3

Hash Keys & Values:      Anna:25        Bert:21        Cleo:27
```

53

Interrupting loops

Perl provides these three keywords that can be used to interrupt the iterations of **for**, **while**, **do while**, and **foreach** loops:

● **last** – immediately exits the loop, makes no further iterations, and moves to the next statement outside the loop (similar to a "break" statement in other programming languages).

● **next** – skips the current iteration, then moves to the next iteration inside the loop (similar to a "continue" statement in other programming languages).

● **redo** – restarts the current iteration, then moves to the beginning of the loop block.

break.pl

1 Begin a Perl program by declaring three scalar variables
```perl
use strict ;
use warnings ;
my ( $i, $j, $input ) ;
```

2 Next, add a loop containing a nested inner loop that outputs the iteration count of each loop
```perl
for ( $i = 1; $i < 4; $i++ ) {
    print "\n" ;
    for ( $j = 1; $j < 4; $j++ ) {
        # Interrupts to be inserted here (Steps 4-6).
        print "Iteration: $i:$j \n" ;
    }
}
```

3 Save the script file as "break.pl", then run the program
perl break.pl

```
C:\Scripts>perl break.pl

Iteration: 1:1
Iteration: 1:2
Iteration: 1:3

Iteration: 2:1
Iteration: 2:2
Iteration: 2:3

Iteration: 3:1
Iteration: 3:2
Iteration: 3:3
```

...cont'd

4 Next, inside the inner loop block, insert a conditional test to completely exit the inner loop on its second iteration

```perl
if ( $i == 1 and $j == 2 ) {
    print "\tLast at 1:2\n" ;
    last ;
}
```

5 Now, insert a conditional test to skip only the second iteration of the inner loop

```perl
if ( $i == 2 and $j == 2 ) {
    print "\tNext at 2:2\n" ;
    next ;
}
```

6 Then, insert a conditional test to halt the second iteration of the inner loop until it receives user input

```perl
if ( $i == 3 and $j == 2 ) {
    print "\tRedo at 3:2 - " ;
    print "Enter text to continue: " ;
    $input = <STDIN> ;
    chomp $input ;
    if ( $input eq " ) {
        redo ;
    }
}
```

Here **<STDIN>** is used to read Standard Input from the keyboard. The built-in **chomp** function removes the trailing newline for the equality comparison.

7 Save the script again, then run the program once more and enter text when requested to see how the inner loop gets interrupted

```
C:\Scripts>perl break.pl

Iteration: 1:1
        Last at 1:2

Iteration: 2:1
        Next at 2:2
Iteration: 2:3

Iteration: 3:1
        Redo at 3:2 - Enter text to continue:
        Redo at 3:2 - Enter text to continue: ok
Iteration: 3:2
Iteration: 3:3
```

Creating references

Perl provides the ability to create a "reference" to any data structure. A reference (similar to a "pointer" in other programming languages) is a scalar data type that contains the memory address of the data structure to which it points.

A pointer reference is created in an assignment by prefixing the data structure being assigned with a \ backslash – for example, to create a reference to a variable with this syntax:

```
$reference = \variable
```

The value contained in the original assigned data structure can be changed by dereferencing the pointer using { } braces, like this:

```
${$scalar-reference}
@{$array-reference}
%{$hash-reference}
```

Perl pointer references provide several programming advantages:

- **Efficient memory use** – avoids copying large structures.

- **Nesting data** – enables multi-level storage (arrays of arrays).

- **Passing data** – easily handles complex data structures.

- **Object-Oriented Programming** – fundamental components.

The **print** function can be used to reveal the memory location and values contained in the original assigned data structure.

PL

point.pl

1. Begin a Perl program by declaring two scalar variables – assigning a numeric value and creating a pointer reference
```
use strict ;
use warnings ;
my $num = 4 ;
my $num_ref = \$num ;
```

2. Next, output the value of the original variable, then output its location, contained in the pointer reference, and output its value by dereferencing the pointer
```
print "\nScalar:  $num \n\n" ;
print "Pointer: $num_ref References: ${$num_ref} \n\n" ;
```

3 Now, assign a new value to the original variable by dereferencing the pointer, then output its location and the new value in the original variable

```
${$num_ref} = $num ** 3 ;
print "Pointer: $num_ref Now References: $num \n\n\n" ;
```

4 Then, declare an array variable and a scalar variable – assigning string values and creating a pointer reference

```
my @arr = ( 'A', 'B', 'C' ) ;
my $arr_ref = \@arr ;
```

5 Next, output the values in the array variable, then output its location and its values by dereferencing the pointer

```
print "Array:\t @arr \n\n" ;
print "Pointer: $arr_ref References: @{$arr_ref} \n\n" ;
```

6 Now, assign new values to the array variable by dereferencing the pointer, then output its location and the new values in the array variable

```
@{$arr_ref} = ( 'X', 'Y', 'Z' ) ;
print "Pointer: $arr_ref Now References: @arr \n" ;
```

7 Save the file in your scripts folder, named as "point.pl", then run this program to see the values output

```
perl point.pl
```

```
C:\Scripts>perl point.pl

Scalar:  4

Pointer: SCALAR(0x27ff8003810) References: 4

Pointer: SCALAR(0x27ff8003810) Now References: 64

Array:   A B C

Pointer: ARRAY(0x27ff8048968) References: A B C

Pointer: ARRAY(0x27ff8048968) Now References: X Y Z
```

Don't forget

The location addresses shown here will, of course, be different on your system.

57

Referencing hashes

A pointer reference to a hash is created in just the same way as for scalar and array variables on page 57. There is, however, a caveat with hash references (**%hash**) as they do not interpolate inside double-quoted strings – unlike scalars (**$scalar**) and arrays (**@array**). This is because the **%** character is used in formatted strings with the **printf** function (see page 39), so allowing hash interpolation could lead to ambiguity. The simple solution is to dereference the hash reference and assign its key value pairs to an array as a list, then output its values.

A **foreach** loop can be used to iterate over all elements in array and hash variables via their pointer reference, and the **->** arrow operator can be used to access their individual elements:

PL

hashref.pl

1 Begin a Perl program by declaring a hash variable, a pointer reference variable, and an array variable
```perl
use strict;
use warnings;
my %set = ( Anna => 1, Bert => 2, Cleo => 3 ) ;
my $set_ref = \%set ;
my @list = %set ;
```

2 Next, output the value of the original hash variable, then output its location from its pointer reference, and output the hash values by dereferencing the pointer into a list
```perl
print "\nHash:\t @list \n\n" ;
@list = %{$set_ref} ;
print "Pointer: $set_ref References: @list \n\n" ;
```

3 Now, assign new values to the original hash variable by dereferencing the pointer, then output its location and the new values in the original variable
```perl
%{$set_ref} = ( Deb => 4, Eve => 5, Fey => 6 ) ;
@list = %set ;
print "Pointer: $set_ref Now References: @list \n" ;
```

4 Then, add a loop to output all key value pairs in the hash variable, with the keys sorted alphabetically
```perl
print "\nKey-Value Pairs: ";
foreach my $key ( sort keys %{$set_ref} ) {
    print "$key = $set_ref->{$key}  " ;
}
```

...cont'd

5 Next, declare an array variable containing a matrix (an array of arrays) and create a pointer reference to the array

```perl
my @mtx = ( [1, 2, 3], [4, 5, 6], [7, 8, 9] ) ;
my $mtx_ref = \@mtx ;
```

6 Now, output all element values in each nested array (i.e. each row of the matrix)

```perl
print "\n\nMatrix:\t @{$mtx_ref->[0]} \n\t " ;
print "@{$mtx_ref->[1]} \n\t @{$mtx_ref->[2]} \n" ;
```

7 Then, add a loop to output all element values in every nested array (i.e. the entire matrix)

```perl
print "\nMatrix Elements: ";
foreach my $row ( @{$mtx_ref} ) {
    foreach my $element ( @$row ) {
        print "$element " ;
    }
}
```

8 Finally, add statements to output one selected element from each row of the matrix

```perl
print "\nElement\t[0][0]: $mtx_ref->[0]->[0]   " ;
print "Element[1][1]: $mtx_ref->[1]->[1]   " ;
print "Element[2][2]: $mtx_ref->[2]->[2] \n" ;
```

9 Save the file in your scripts folder, named as "hashref.pl", then run this program to see the values output

```
perl hashref.pl
```

The **->** arrow operator is alternatively called the "dereference operator" when used to access elements of a reference (as it is here) or as the "member operator" when it is used to access class members in Object-Oriented Programming (see Chapter 7).

```
C:\Scripts>perl hashref.pl

Hash:    Anna 1 Bert 2 Cleo 3

Pointer: HASH(0x13d3b6c3b60) References: Anna 1 Bert 2 Cleo 3

Pointer: HASH(0x13d3b6c3b60) Now References: Eve 5 Deb 4 Fey 6

Key-Value Pairs: Deb = 4  Eve = 5  Fey = 6

Matrix:  1 2 3
         4 5 6
         7 8 9

Matrix Elements: 1 2 3 4 5 6 7 8 9
Element[0][0]: 1    Element[1][1]: 5    Element[2][2]: 9
```

Summary

- The **if** keyword evaluates a given expression for a Boolean value of true.

- An **else** statement block can be appended after an **if** block to offer alternative statements to execute when an **if** test is false.

- One or more **elsif** blocks can be appended after an **if** block to offer alternative conditional tests and statements to execute.

- The **unless** keyword evaluates a given expression for a Boolean value of false – the opposite of an **if** conditional test.

- A **for** loop has a counter and a conditional test, and will repeatedly execute its statements until the test becomes false.

- A **while** loop has a conditional test and will repeatedly execute its statements until the test becomes false.

- A **do while** loop will always execute its statements once and will repeat until its conditional test becomes false.

- An **until** loop has a conditional test and will repeatedly execute its statements until the test becomes true.

- A **foreach** loop will iterate over all values in an array or all values in a list.

- The **foreach** loop assigns each value in turn to a named scalar variable or to the default special **$_** variable.

- The **last** keyword is used to immediately exit a loop.

- The **next** keyword is used to exit the current loop iteration.

- The **redo** keyword is used to restart the current iteration.

- A reference is a scalar data type that contains the memory address of the data structure to which it points.

- A reference is created in an assignment by prefixing the data structure being assigned with a \ backslash.

- Unlike scalar and array references, the **%** character prevents hash reference interpolation in double-quoted strings.

- The **->** arrow operator can be used to access individual elements of array references and hash references.

4 Handling Strings

Adjusting strings

Perl provides operators and functions that can be used to make simple adjustments to strings:

- **.** – the full stop operator performs string concatenation. It joins two strings together to form one single string.

- **.=** – the string concatenation assignment operator appends a string to an existing string, modifying the original value.

- **x** – this operator performs string repetition. It repeats a string (or list) a specified number of times. This is useful to output a line of repeated characters.

- **q( )** – this provides an alternative way to enclose a string within ' ' single quotes. It is useful to include a single quote within a double-quoted string, without the \' escape sequence.

- **qq( )** – this provides an alternative way to enclose a string within " " double quotes. It is particularly useful to allow the inclusion of variables and escape sequences for interpolation.

- **qx( )** – this provides an alternative way to enclose a string within ` ` backticks. It is used to execute system commands and it also supports interpolation, as with double quotes.

- **qw( )** – this provides an alternative way to create a list of words without the need for individual quotes and commas. It is useful to initialize an array of words.

adjust.pl

1 Begin a Perl program by declaring and initializing a scalar variable containing a string value
```perl
use strict ;
use warnings ;
my $mode = 'Fabulous' ;
```

2 Next, assign a double-quoted string that allows interpolation to another variable, then output the value
```perl
my $show = qq( \nAbsolutely $mode ) ;
print $show ;
```

3 Now, assign a single-quoted string containing an internal single quote to a variable, then output the value within a double-quoted string
```perl
my $cast = q( Eddy & Eddy's friend Patsy. ) ;
print "\nStars: $cast \n" ;
```

4 Adjust the original variable's string value, using concatenation to add an escaped newline prefix and an additional string suffix, then output the adjusted string

```
$mode = "\n".$mode." Lifestyle" ;
print $mode ;
```

5 Next, concatenate and assign a further string to the adjusted string, then output the new value

```
$mode .= ": On a Budget\n" ;
print $mode ;
```

6 Now, output a line by repeating a hyphen character 60 times within multiple arguments passed for printing

```
print "\n", '-' x 60 ,"\n" ;
```

7 Then, assign a PowerShell command to a variable (or any valid command-line command) enclosed in ` ` backticks or the **qx( )** function for execution, then output the captured result

```
my $langs = qx( PowerShell Get-InstalledLanguage ) ;
print $langs ;
```

8 Save the file, then run the program – to see the adjusted strings in output

```
C:\Scripts>perl adjust.pl

Absolutely Fabulous
Stars: Eddy & Eddy's friend Patsy.

Fabulous Lifestyle
Fabulous Lifestyle: On a Budget

_____

Language Language Packs  Language Features
_____ _____   _____

el-GR    LXP             BasicTyping, OCR
en-US    LpCab           BasicTyping, Handwriting, Speech,
                         TextToSpeech, OCR
fr-FR    LpCab, LXP      BasicTyping, OCR
```

Hot tip

The commas here are separating three arguments, which the **print** function processes in turn and outputs them sequentially.

Don't forget

The PowerShell result will vary depending on which languages are installed on your system.

63

Manipulating strings

Perl provides functions that can be used to manipulate strings:

- **chomp** – removes the trailing newline from the end of a string. This is useful to trim user input (see page 51).

- **chop** – removes the last character of a string.

- **length** – returns the number of characters in a string, including any space characters.

- **reverse** – reverses the order of characters in a string.

- **lc** – converts all characters in a string to lowercase.

- **lcfirst** – converts the first character in a string to lowercase.

- **uc** – converts all characters in a string to uppercase.

- **ucfirst** – converts the first character in a string to uppercase.

- **split** – splits a string into a list of substrings based on a specified delimiter pattern and up to an optional maximum number of splits. The split function has this syntax:

split / *delimiter-pattern* /, *string-to-split*, *maximum-splits*

- **join** – concatenates a list of strings into a single string with each string separated by a specified separator, with this syntax:

join *separator*, *list-of-strings-to-join*

manipulate.pl

1 Begin a Perl program by declaring and initializing two scalar variables containing a string value and its length
```
use strict ;
use warnings ;
my $word= 'drawers' ;
my $len = length $word ;
```

2 Next, output the string value and the string length
```
print "\nOriginal: $word ($len) \n" ;
```

3 Now, remove the final character from the string, then output its new value and new length
```
chop $word ;
$len = length $word ;
print "Chopped:  $word ($len) \n" ;
```

4 Then, reverse the string and output its manipulated value
```perl
$word = reverse $word ;
print "Reversed: $word \n\n" ;
```

5 Next, manipulate the string case and output the changes
```perl
$word = ucfirst $word ;
print "Sentence case: $word \n" ;
$word = uc $word ;
print "Uppercase: $word \n\n" ;
```

6 Now, assign a comma-separated list to a scalar variable, then split it into an array and output its elements
```perl
my $basket = ( 'Apple, Banana, Cherry' ) ;
my @fruits = split /,/, $basket ;
print "Fruits: @fruits \n" ;
```

7 Change the value of an array element, then unite all array elements and output them in a single string
```perl
@fruits[0] = 'Apricot' ;
$basket = join ' | ', @fruits ;
print "Fruits now: $basket \n" ;
```

8 Save the file, then run the program – to see the manipulated strings in output

```
Command Prompt

C:\Scripts>perl manipulate.pl

Original: drawers (7)
Chopped:  drawer (6)
Reversed: reward

Sentence case: Reward
Uppercase: REWARD

Fruits: Apple Banana Cherry
Fruits now: Apricot | Banana | Cherry
```

Hot tip

It is useful to convert strings to a single case when making comparisons in an expression.

Extracting substrings

Perl provides functions to seek a substring within strings:

● **substr** – extracts a substring from a string, beginning at a specified character position and ending after the final character in the string. The basic syntax of this function looks like this:

substr *string-to-search, position*

Optionally, the number of characters to be extracted from the string can be specified as length value with this syntax:

substr *string-to-search, position, length*

Additionally, a value can be specified to replace the extracted substring with this syntax:

substr *string-to-search, position, length, replacement*

● **index** – returns the starting position within a string of the first occurrence of a specified substring, or returns **-1** if the substring is not found. Its syntax looks like this:

index *string-to-search, substring-to-find*

Optionally, the starting position of a search can be specified:

index *string-to-search, substring-to-find, starting-position*

● **rindex** – returns the starting position within a string of the last occurrence of a specified substring, or returns **-1** if the substring is not found. Its syntax provides the same options as those of the **index** function.

PL

substring.pl

1 Begin a Perl program by declaring and initializing a scalar variable containing a string value, and declare three more scalar variables
```perl
use strict ;
use warnings ;
my $string = 'To be or not to be, that is the question.' ;
my ( $substring, $len, $pos ) ;
```

2 Next, output the string value and the string length
```perl
$len = length $string ;
print "\n$string ($len) \n" ;
```

3 Now, extract a substring of 9 characters length and starting at position 9 in the original string
```perl
$substring = substr $string, 9, 9 ;
$len = length $substring ;
print "$substring ($len) \n" ;
```

4 Then, extract a substring starting at position 20 in the original string and up to the end of the string
```perl
$substring = substr $string, 20 ;
$len = length $substring ;
print "$substring ($len) \n\n" ;
```

5 Now, search the string to seek the starting position of the first and last occurrence of a substring
```perl
$pos = index $string, 'be' ;
print "First 'be' at position: $pos \n" ;
$pos = rindex $string, 'be' ;
print "Last 'be' at position: $pos \n\n" ;
```

6 Next, seek another substring – that may be absent
```perl
$substring = 'Hamlet' ;
$pos = index $string, $substring ;
if ($pos == -1) { print "String $substring not found.\n"; }
```

7 Then, replace a substring with a new longer value
```perl
substr $string, 28, 4, 'a vital ' ;
print "$string \n" ;
```

8 Save the file, then run the program to see the substrings

```
Command Prompt                              □   ×

C:\Scripts>perl substring.pl

To be or not to be, that is the question. (41)
not to be (9)
that is the question. (21)

First 'be' at position: 3
Last 'be' at position: 16
String 'Hamlet' not found.

To be or not to be, that is a vital question.
```

Hot tip

Notice that code blocks that contain only a single statement may be written on one line.

Modifying strings

Parts of a string can be replaced using the Perl **s///** substitution operator, which has this syntax:

s/ *pattern* / *replacement* /

The basic substitution operation simply replaces the first occurrence of the specified pattern with the specified replacement. The resulting modified string can then be assigned to a variable using the Perl **=~** "binding operator". Optionally, modifiers can be suffixed after the **s///** substitution operator to alter its behavior:

- **g** – global substitution will replace all occurrences of the pattern with the specified replacement.

- **i** – insensitive substitution will replace the pattern in either lowercase or uppercase with the specified replacement.

- **r** – return substitution will return the modified string without changing the original.

The modifiers can be combined. For example, **s///gi** will perform global insensitive replacement.

Specific characters in a string can be replaced using the Perl **tr///** translation operator, which has this syntax:

tr/ *search-list* / *replacement-list* /

The basic translation operation replaces all characters in the specified search list with those in the specified replacement list. The resulting modified string can then be assigned to a variable using the Perl **=~** binding operator. Optionally, modifiers can be suffixed after the **tr///** translation operator to alter its behavior:

- **c** – complement translation will replace all characters in the search list with characters in the replacement list.

- **d** – delete translation will delete all characters in the search list without specified characters in the replacement list.

- **s** – squash translation will delete all duplicate sequential characters without specified characters in the replacement list.

The **tr///** translation operator can also be used to count the number of times the characters in the search list appear within a string when no replacement character is specified.

Don't forget

The distinction to recognize between the substitution operation and the translation operation is that the **s///** operator works at string level and the **tr///** operator works at character level.

...cont'd

1 Begin a Perl program by declaring and initializing a scalar variable containing a string and output its value

```
use strict ;
use warnings ;
my $string = 'Hello World!' ;
print "\nOriginal:\t $string" ;
```

modify.pl

2 Next, assign a case-insensitive search replacement to another variable and output both variable values

```
my $var = $string =~ s/world/Mike/ri ;
print "\nInterim:\t $var \tOriginal: $string" ;
```

3 Now, assign a case-insensitive search replacement to the original string and output its value

```
$string =~ s/world/Perl/i ;
print "\nModified:\t $string" ;
```

4 Then, assign a well-known quotation to replace the modified string and output its new value

```
$string = 'Keep Calm and Carry On.' ;
print "\n\nQuote: $string" ;
```

5 Next, replace all lowercase vowel characters in the quotation with an * asterisk character for each one

```
$string =~ tr/aeiou/*/ ;
print "\nEdit:  $string" ;
```

6 Finally, count the number of times the asterisk character appears in the string and output the total

```
$var = $string =~ tr/*// ;
print "\nCount: $var \n" ;
```

7 Save the file, then run the program to see modifications

```
C:\Scripts>perl modify.pl

Original:       Hello World!
Interim:        Hello Mike!      Original: Hello World!
Modified:       Hello Perl!

Quote: Keep Calm and Carry On.
Edit:  K**p C*lm *nd C*rry On.   Count: 5
```

Matching patterns

A string can be searched for a specified substring pattern using the Perl **m//** "match operator". The match operation returns **1** when the substring is found, otherwise it returns **0**. Modifiers **g** (global) and **i** (insensitive) can be suffixed after the **m//** match operator. The search result can be assigned to a variable using the Perl **=~** binding operator, as with the **s///** and **tr///** operators. The **m//** match operator captures the last matched group in read-only variables:

- **$&** – the entire matched substring.

- **$`** – everything before the matched substring.

- **$'** – everything after the matched substring.

The substring can be specified simply as a character sequence or as a "regular expression". The topic of regular expressions is extensive and goes beyond the scope of this book, but it is useful to understand how they can be used with the **m//** match operator:

- **.*** – matches any sequence of characters.

- **$** – signifies the end of a string to ensure the pattern matches only if it appears at the end of the searched string.

- **\$** – matches a literal dollar sign (escaped).

- **.** – wildcard matches any single character except a newline.

- **\.** – matches a literal full stop (escaped).

- **^** – signifies the start of a string to ensure the pattern matches only if it appears at the start of the searched string.

- **\d+** – matches one or more digits 0-9 (as on page 179).

- **\w+** – matches one or more word characters (a-z, A-Z, 0-9, and _ the underscore character).

- **\w{2, }** – matches at least two word characters.

- **@** – matches a literal @ symbol.

- **[ ]** – signifies a "character class" to match a specific set of characters specified inside the square brackets.

- **( )** – captures matches into read-only variables **$1**, **$2**, etc.

...cont'd

1 Begin a Perl program by declaring and initializing a scalar variable containing a string and output its value

```perl
use strict ;
use warnings ;
my $string = 'Sugar and Spice' ;
print "\n$string" ;
```

match.pl

2 Seek a match for the string "and", then output the results

```perl
$string =~ m/and/ ;
print "\nMatch: '".$&."'\tBefore: '".$`."'  After: '".$'."'\n" ;
```

3 Seek a match for two more strings and output the results

```perl
print $string =~ m/sp.*/i ? "Found 'sp'.\n" : "Absent 'sp'.\n" ;
print $string =~ m/ps.*/i ? "Found 'ps'.\n" : "Absent 'ps'.\n" ;
```

4 Next, extract a monetary substring from a string

```perl
$string = "Reduced to only \$7.99." ;
$string =~  /(\$\d+\.\d+)/g ;
print "\nPrice:\t $& \n\n" ;
```

5 Now, add a loop to request and validate an email address

```perl
do {
    print 'Enter your Email address: ' ;
    $string = <STDIN> ;
    chomp $string ;
} while ( $string !~ /^([\w\.-]+)@\w+\.\w{2,}$/ ) ;
print "Valid Email address for $1.\n" ;
```

The **do while** loop used here to get user input is similar to the loop described on page 51.

6 Save the file, then run the program to see matches

```
Command Prompt  ×   + ∨                              –  □  ✕

C:\Scripts>perl match.pl

Sugar and Spice
Match: 'and'     Before: 'Sugar '  After: ' Spice'
Found 'sp'.
Absent 'ps'.

Price:   $7.99

Enter your Email address: mike@example
Enter your Email address: mike@example.com
Valid Email address for mike.
```

Building date strings

The Perl **DateTime** module allows date and time strings to be easily constructed. To make this available in a Perl program, a **use DateTime** pragma must be included in the script.

A **DateTime** object can be created for the current time or you can build a custom date and time. The **DateTime** object contains many "get" and "set" methods (functions), which can be referenced using the **->** operator and **=>** operator respectively. Some of the most commonly used methods are listed in the table below:

UTC (Coordinated Universal Time) is the global standard time. It does not change during periods of daylight saving time.

Method	Returns
now	Current date and time (UTC default) e.g. **2027-12-25T17:45:30**.
new	Date and time at the start of a specified year e.g. **2030-01-01T00:00:00**.
time_zone	Timezone information hash. Current timezone if set as **'local'**.
mdy	Date in **Month-Day-Year** format.
dmy	Date in **Day-Month-Year** format.
year	Year in **YYYY** format.
month	Month number **1-12**.
month_name	Full month name (e.g. **January**).
month_abbr	Abbreviated month name (e.g. **Jan**).
day	Day number **1-31**.
day_name	Full day name (e.g. **Monday**).
day_abbr	Abbreviated day name (e.g. **Mon**).
hms	Time in **HH:MM:SS** format.
hour	Hour **0-23**.
minute	Minute **0-59**.
second	Second **0-59**.
am_or_pm	Appropriate localized **AM** or **PM**.
time_zone_long_name	Full timezone name e.g. **Asia/Tokyo**.
time_zone_short_name	Abbreviated timezone name e.g. **JST** (Japan Standard Time).

1 Begin a Perl program by importing the **DateTime** module
```
use strict ;
use warnings ;
use DateTime ;
```

PL

datetime.pl

2 Next, build an object for the current local date and time
```
my $dt = DateTime->now( time_zone=>'local' ) ;
my ($d, $m) = ( $dt->day_name, $dt->month_name ) ;
my ($n, $h) = ( $dt->day, $dt->hour ) ;
my ($x, $w) = ( $dt->minute, $dt->am_or_pm ) ;
my ($y, $z) = ( $dt->year, $dt->time_zone_long_name ) ;
```

3 Output the object, plus formatted date and time strings
```
print "\nDateTime Now:\t $dt " ;
print "\nDate Now:\t $d, $m $n, $y " ;
print "\nTime Now:\t $h:$x $w - $z " ;
```

4 Now, build and output an object for a future date and time
```
$dt = DateTime->new(
   year => 2027, month => 12, day => 6,
   hour => 23, minute => 15, second => 30,
   time_zone => 'America/Los_Angeles'
) ;
print "\n\nDateTime Set:\t $dt " ;
```

5 Then, create a formatted version of the future date and time, then output the formatted string
```
($d, $h, $x) = ( $dt->mdy('/'), $dt->hour, $dt->minute ) ;
$z = $dt->time_zone_short_name;
print "\nFormatted Set:\t $d $h:$x $z \n" ;
```

Beware

DateTime strings are unlike regular strings but can be converted to a regular string using a **DateTime** object's **stringify** method.

6 Save the file, then run the program to see the date and time strings

```
Command Prompt   X    +   v                     —    □    ×

C:\Scripts>perl datetime.pl

DateTime Now:    2025-05-13T11:45:49
Date Now:        Tuesday, May 13, 2025
Time Now:        11:45 AM – Europe/Athens

DateTime Set:    2027-12-06T23:15:30
Formatted Set:   12/06/2027 23:15 PST
```

Formatting strings

The Perl **printf** function can usefully format a value for output by inserting a format specifier within a string. This acts as a placeholder for the actual value that is specified after the string. Multiple format specifiers can be included within a string, and the actual values specified as a comma-separated list after the string.

Similarly, there is also a **sprintf** function that performs formatting in exactly the same way as the **printf** function, but this returns the formatted string for storage rather than directly printing it out.

Commonly used format specifiers are listed in the table below:

Specifier	Output Format
%s	A character string.
%-10s	A character string left-justified in a field width of 10 characters.
%d	An integer number.
%+d	A positive integer number prefixed with a + sign.
%0d	A signed integer padded with leading zeros.
%05d	A signed integer padded with leading zeros if needed and at least 5 digits wide.
%f	A floating-point number.
%5f	A floating-point number in a field width of at least 5 characters.
%5.2f	A floating-point number in a field width of at least 5 characters and with 2 decimal places.
%b	A binary (base-2) number.
%04b	A binary number with leading zeros if needed and at least 4 digits wide (1 nibble).
%08b	A binary number with leading zeros if needed and at least 8 digits wide (1 byte).
%x	A hexadecimal (base-16) number in lowercase.
%X	A hexadecimal number in uppercase.
0x%X	A hexadecimal number with the 0x prefix.
0x%p	A pointer memory address with the 0x prefix.
%o	An octal (base-8) number.

1 Begin a Perl program by declaring and initializing one string and one reference variable

```perl
use strict ;
use warnings ;
my $name = 'Susan' ;
my $name_ref = \$name ;
```

format.pl

2 Next, output formatted strings

```perl
printf "\nHello, %s !\n", 'Mike' ;
printf "Welcome, %s !\n", $name ;
```

3 Output formatted integer and floating-point numbers

```perl
printf "You have %d new messages. \n", 7 ;
printf "James Bond: %03d \n", 7 ;
printf "Value of Pi = %f \n", 3.141593 ;
printf "Remaining balance: \$%4.2f\ \n", 132.50 ;
```

4 Now, output formatted binary and hexadecimal numbers

```perl
printf "Byte for decimal 107: %08b \n", 107 ;
printf "Nibble of decimal 13: %04b \n", 13 ;
printf "Hexadecimal of decimal 10: %x \n", 10 ;
printf "HTML Red: 0x%X0000 \n", 255 ;
```

5 Then, store and output a pointer memory address

```perl
$name = sprintf "String location: 0x%p \n", $name_ref ;
print $name ;
```

6 Save the file, then run the program to see the formatted output

```
Command Prompt  ×  +  ˅                    —  □  ×

C:\Scripts>perl format.pl

Hello, Mike !
Welcome, Susan !
You have 7 new messages.
James Bond: 007
Value of Pi = 3.141593
Remaining balance: $132.50
Byte for decimal 107: 01101011
Nibble of decimal 13: 1101
Hexadecimal of decimal 10: a
HTML Red: 0xFF0000
String location: 0x21b8e7b4430
```

Summary

- The full stop . operator performs concatenation, and the **x** operator performs repetition.

- The **q( )**, **qq( )**, **qw( )**, and **qx( )** operators perform quotation.

- Strings can be manipulated with the functions **chomp**, **chop**, **lc**, **lcfirst**, **uc**, **ucfirst**, **length**, **reverse**, **split**, and **join**.

- Substrings within strings can be sought using the functions **substr**, **index**, and **rindex**.

- Parts of a string can be replaced using the **s///** substitution operator and its **g**, **i**, and **r** modifiers.

- Characters in a string can be replaced using the **tr///** translation operator and its **c**, **d**, and **s** modifiers.

- Modified strings can be assigned to a variable using the **=~** binding operator.

- A string can be searched for a specified substring pattern using the **m//** match operator.

- The **m//** match operator will return **1** if its specified pattern is matched or **0** if no match is found.

- The **m//** match operator captures the last matched group in read-only variables **$&**, **$`**, and **$'**.

- The substring pattern given to the **m//** match operator can be specified as a character sequence or as a regular expression.

- The **DateTime** module contains functions that allow date and time strings to be constructed.

- **DateTime** "get" functions are referenced by the **->** operator and its "set" functions are referenced by the **=>** operator.

- The **printf** function formats a value for output by inserting a format specifier within a string.

- The **sprintf** function formats a value for storage by inserting a format specifier within a string.

- Common format specifiers used with the **printf** and **sprintf** functions are **%s**, **%d**, **%f**, **%b**, **%x**, **%o**, and **%p**.

5 Structuring Programs

This chapter demonstrates how to create your own custom functions, packages, and modules.

Creating subroutines

Previous examples in this book have used built-in functions of the Perl language, such as the **print** function, but most Perl programs also contain a number of programmer-defined custom functions that can be called as required when the program runs.

In Perl, a custom function is called a "subroutine" and is created using the **sub** keyword followed by a valid name of your choice and a pair of **{ }** braces. The opening **{** brace should appear on the same line as the name. Statements to be executed whenever the function is called should appear on subsequent lines to form the function body with a four-space indentation. The closing **}** brace should appear on the line following the function body without indentation. The subroutine syntax therefore looks like this:

```
sub subroutine-function-name {
    statement-to-be-executed
    statement-to-be-executed
}
```

Once the function statements have been executed by calling the function name followed by **( )** parentheses, program flow resumes at the point directly following the function call. This modularity is very useful in Perl programming to isolate set routines so that they can be called upon repeatedly.

To create custom functions it is necessary to recognize the accessibility ("scope") of variables in a program:

● Variables created outside functions can be referenced by statements inside functions – they have "global" scope.

● Variables created inside functions cannot be referenced from outside the function in which they have been created – these have "local" scope.

The limited accessibility of local variables means that variables of the same name can appear in different functions without conflict.

Variables within a function body are initialized afresh each time the function gets called. Their value can, however, be made to persist by declaring the variable with the special **state** keyword. This requires a **use feature** pragma be included in the program specifying a **state** feature – alternatively specified as **q(state)**.

The Perl, **my**, **local**, and **our** keywords control variable scope within a program – as described on page 24.

1 Begin a Perl program by including the **state** feature

```perl
use strict ;
use warnings ;
use feature q(state) ;
```

subroutine.pl

2 Next, initialize a variable that will be accessible from anywhere within this program and output its value

```perl
my $global_str = "\nGlobal Scope: 0\n" ;
print "\n $global_str \n" ;
```

3 Now, add a subroutine containing a variable that will be only accessible from within this function

```perl
sub repeat {
    my $num = 1 ;
    print "\tLocal Scope: $num \n" ;
    $num++ ;
}
```

Hot tip

This incrementer serves no purpose, as the incremented variable value is never used.

4 Then, add a subroutine containing a **state** variable that will be only accessible from within this function

```perl
sub count {
    state $num = 1 ;
    if ( $num == 1 ) { print "\n $global_str \n"; }
    print "\tLocal State: $num \n" ;
    $num++ ;
}
```

5 Finally, call each of the subroutines three times to output their variable values and the global variable value once

```perl
for (1..3) { repeat( ) ; }
for (1..3) { count( ) ; }
```

6 Save the file, then run the program to compare the output from calls to the custom subroutine functions

```
Command Prompt  ×     +  ∨          —   □   ×

C:\Scripts>perl subroutine.pl

Global Scope: 0
        Local Scope: 1  Local Scope: 1  Local Scope: 1
Global Scope: 0
        Local State: 1  Local State: 2  Local State: 3
```

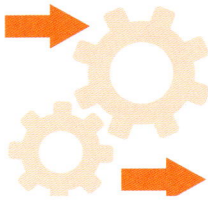

Passing arguments

Invariably, subroutines are passed values by the caller for use by statements within the subroutine's body. These are specified in the parentheses that follow the subroutine's name in the calling statement. Multiple values can be specified as a comma-separated list, and are known as "arguments" being passed to the subroutine:

subroutine-function-name(argument-1, argument-2)

The arguments passed to a subroutine function are received by a special @_ "parameter array". Individual elements can be referenced by their index number using @_[0], @_[1], etc.

For better readability, a @_ parameter array element can be assigned to a scalar variable individually, like this:

my $variable-name = @_[0]

Multiple @_ parameter array elements can be assigned, in order, to a comma-separated list of scalar variables:

my ($variable-name1, $variable-name2) = @_

After executing the statements within the subroutine function body, a value can be sent back to the caller by specifying the value in a final statement using the Perl **return** keyword. The syntax of the subroutine might then look like this:

```
sub subroutine-function-name {
    my ($variable-name1, $variable-name2) = @_
    statements-to-be-executed
    return value
}
```

Optionally, the **return** keyword can also be used without specifying a value in order to simply exit the function.

Subroutines can be made more flexible by checking that the number of arguments being passed by the caller matches the number of receiving variables specified in the subroutine. When fewer arguments are passed, a **0** default can be provided, either by an **unless defined** statement or more concisely by assignment using the Perl **//** defined-or operator:

$variable-name3 = 0 unless defined $variable-name3

$variable-name3 //= 0

Beware

A single passed argument can be assigned to a variable with **my ($var) = @_** but remember that the variable must be enclosed in parentheses as a list context.

...cont'd

1 Begin a Perl program by declaring just one variable
```perl
use strict ;
use warnings ;
my $result ;
```

args.pl

2 Next, add a subroutine to receive a single argument
```perl
sub square {
    my ( $num ) = @_ ;
    return $num * $num ;
}
```

3 Now, add a subroutine to receive two arguments
```perl
sub raise {
    my ( $num1, $num2 ) = @_ ;
    return $num1 ** $num2 ;
}
```

4 Then, add a subroutine to receive two or three arguments
```perl
sub sum {
    my ( $num1, $num2, $num3 ) = @_ ;
    $num3 //= 0 ;
    return $num1 + $num2 + $num3 ;
}
```

5 Finally, call each of the subroutines and output their returns
```perl
$result = square(2) ;
print "\nSquare 2:\t $result " ;

$result = raise(2, 4) ;
print "\nRaise 2 ^ 4:\t $result " ;

$result = sum(2, 4);
print "\nSum 2 + 4:\t $result " ;
print "\nSum 2 + 4 + 6:\t".sum(2, 4, 6)."\n" ;
```

Hot tip

Notice that the returned value can be directly inserted into a concatenated string.

6 Save the file, then run the program to see the output from calls to the custom subroutine functions

```
Command Prompt ×    +  ˅                    —   □   ×

C:\Scripts>perl args.pl
Square 2:       4
Raise 2 ^ 4:    16
Sum 2 + 4:      6
Sum 2 + 4 + 6:  12
```

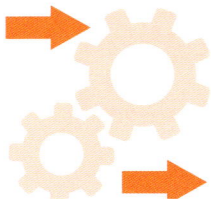

Passing lists

Lists and arrays are simply a collection of scalar values, so they can be passed to the @_ parameter array in subroutines and Perl will extract each value into a separate element.

There is, however, a potential problem to be aware of when passing a mixture of scalars and a list to a subroutine. If a list argument is passed before the scalars, Perl's argument-flattening process will merge all elements into a single array without respect to the order in which the arguments were passed. It is therefore important in this case to always pass the list as the final argument to maintain the order of the list items.

PL

list_args.pl

1 Begin a Perl program by declaring and initializing two scalar variables and an array variable containing a list

```
use strict ;
use warnings ;
my $str = "\nList..." ;
my $num = 2 ;
my @arr = (4, 6, 8) ;
```

2 Next, add a subroutine to receive all arguments and output each one in a concatenated string

```
sub extract {
    my @items = @_ ;
    print join("\n", @items), "\n" ;
}
```

3 Now, add calls to the subroutine, passing all the variable values as arguments in incorrect order and in correct order

```
extract( @arr, $str, $num ) ;
extract( $str, $num, @arr ) ;
```

4 Save the file, then run the program to see the output from calls to the custom subroutine function

```
C:\Scripts>perl list_args.pl
4       6       8
List ... 2

List ... 2       4       6       8
```

Passing hashes

When passing a hash to a subroutine, Perl will flatten the key-value pairs into a sequential list. This means that the subroutine would need to re-establish their associations.

A more efficient way to pass hash arguments, which preserves the key-value associations, is to pass a reference to the hash as an argument to the subroutine. In this case, the first element of the @_ parameter array will contain the memory address of the hash. The Perl built-in **shift** function can be used to remove this and assign it to a scalar – to allow access to the hash keys and values.

1 Begin a Perl program by declaring and initializing a hash variable and a scalar variable containing a reference
```perl
use strict ;
use warnings ;
my %hash = (A => 'Assembly', B => 'Bash', C => 'C++') ;
my $hash_ref = \%hash ;
```

hash_args.pl

2 Next, add a subroutine to output the hash memory address and a list of key-value pairs
```perl
sub extract_by_ref {
    my $ref = shift ;
    print "\nAddress: $ref \n" ;
    for my $key ( sort keys %$ref ) {
        print "$key : $ref->{$key} \n" ;
    }
}
```

3 Now, add a call to the subroutine, passing the reference to the hash as an argument to output key-value pairs
```perl
print extract_by_ref( $hash_ref ) ;
```

4 Save the file, then run the program to see the output from the call to the custom subroutine function

```
C:\Scripts>perl hash_args.pl

Address: HASH(0x1df5c3c3c30)
A : Assembly
B : Bash
C : C++
```

Packaging code

Perl functions can be packaged to prevent conflicts between variable and function names. This is especially useful in larger projects that may contain lots of code. Perl packages can be imported into scripts for use in multiple Perl programs.

A Perl package begins with the Perl **package** keyword followed by a name of your choice. The package name defines a namespace with unique scope, and by convention should use CamelCase, such as "MyPackage". The name is followed by the usual **use strict** and **use warnings** pragmas to enforce good coding practice. A package defines a unique namespace, so a script can contain multiple packages to organize the code or be created as a custom module.

The package can next define one or more subroutine functions, then must always end with a **1** statement, returning true to confirm to the Perl interpreter that the package has loaded.

Compound.pm

1 Begin a Perl package by specifying "Compound" as the package namespace, then add the usual pragmas
```perl
package Compound ;

use strict ;
use warnings ;
```

2 Next, add a subroutine to receive all arguments and return the result after performing simple arithmetic
```perl
sub calculate_cost {
    my ( $loan, $rate, $term ) = @_ ;
    return $loan * ( (1 + $rate) ** $term ) ;
}
```

3 Now, add a final statement to confirm that the package has loaded
```perl
1 ;
```

4 Then, create a new subfolder named "MyModules" within the "Scripts" folder

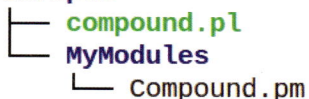

```
Scripts
├── compound.pl
└── MyModules
        └── Compound.pm
```

5 Finally, save the package file in the new subfolder as a file named "Compound.pm" (<u>P</u>erl <u>M</u>odule)

In order for a Perl script to make use of the functions defined within a custom Perl module, the script code must specify its location in a **use lib** pragma, stating its directory folder path within quotes, and must specify the package name in a **use** statement.

To call package functions, the function name must be prefixed by the package name and a :: double colon, like this:

Package-name::subroutine-function-name(*arguments-list*)

6 Begin a Perl program by specifying the location of the folder containing a package, and the package name itself

```
use strict ;
use warnings ;
use lib qw(./MyModules) ;
use Compound ;
```

compound.pl

7 Next, declare and initialize three scalar variables

```
my ( $loan, $rate, $term ) = ( 1000. 0.05, 10 ) ;
```

8 Now, pass the variable values as arguments to a function in the specified package and assign the returned value

```
my $cost = Compound::calculate_cost($loan, $rate, $term) ;
```

9 Then, output the variable values and the returned value

```
printf "\nLoan amount: \$%.2f", $loan ;
printf "\nAnnual interest rate: %.2f%%", ($rate * 100) ;
printf "\nCost after %d years: \$%.2f \n", $term, $cost ;
```

10 Save the file in the Scripts folder, then run the program to see the output from the package subroutine function

```
C:\Scripts>perl compound.pl

Loan amount: $1000.00
Annual interest rate: 5.00%
Cost after 10 years: $1628.89
```

Exporting symbols

A Perl module is a reusable component that can contain multiple packages. Subroutine functions can be exported from a package into a script, so they can be used by the script without the need to prefix the function name with the package name.

The package first needs to include a **use Exporter 'import'** pragma, allowing it to export package function symbols and import them into the script's namespace. The symbols to be exported can then be specified to an **our @EXPORT_OK** array. For efficiency, this will only export the symbols of subroutine functions that the script explicitly states to be required.

Calibrate.pm

1 Begin a Perl package by specifying "Calibrate" as the package namespace, then add the usual pragmas
```
package Calibrate ;

use strict ;
use warnings ;
```

2 Next, add statements allowing the export of symbols for subroutine functions named "F2C" and "C2F"
```
use Exporter 'import' ;
use @EXPORT_OK = qw(F2C C2F) ;
```

3 Now, add the subroutine functions to receive an argument and return the result after performing simple arithmetic
```
sub F2C {
    my ( $temperature ) = @_ ;
    return ( $temperature  - 32 ) / 1.8 ;
}

sub C2F {
    my ( $temperature ) = @_ ;
    return ( $temperature * 1.8 ) + 32 ;
}
```

4 Now, add a final statement to confirm that the package has loaded
```
1 ;
```

5 Then, save the package file in the "MyModules" subfolder as a file named "Calibrate.pm"

Hot tip

Symbols are names that represent variables, functions, or other items in a namespace.

In order for a Perl script to make use of the functions allowed to be exported from a custom Perl module, the script code must specify its location in a **use lib** pragma, stating its directory folder path within quotes. It must also specify the package name in a **use** statement together with a quoted list of the function names.

```
use Package-name qw( function-name function-name )
```

6 Begin a Perl program by specifying the location of the package folder, the package name, and function names
```perl
use strict ;
use warnings ;

use lib qw(./MyModules) ;
use Calibrate qw(F2C C2F) ;
```

calibrate.pl

7 Next, declare a scalar variable
```perl
my $temperature ;
```

8 Now, request user input, then output a converted value
```perl
print "\nEnter Fahrenheit: " ;
$temperature = <STDIN> ;
chomp $temperature ;
print "$temperature F is ".F2C($temperature)." C\n" ;
```

9 Again, request user input, then output a converted value
```perl
print "\nEnter Celsius: " ;
$temperature = <STDIN> ;
chomp $temperature ;
print "$temperature C is ".C2F($temperature)." F\n" ;
```

10 Save the file in the Scripts folder, then run the program and enter values to see output from package functions

The **use** keyword loads a module at compile time. There is a **require** keyword alternative that loads a module at run time, but **use** is typically used more often as it will detect errors earlier.

```
Command Prompt

C:\Scripts>perl calibrate.pl

Enter Fahrenheit: 98.6
98.6 F is 37 C

Enter Celsius: 37
37 C is 98.6 F
```

Deploying modules

Custom Perl modules can be packaged as compressed "tarball" archives (in **tar.gz** format) for sharing and deployment.

1 Install a module starter kit with this command
Scripts> **cpan Module::Starter**
– *this will provide ready-made templates*

2 Create a module for the custom "Calibrate" example on page 87
Scripts> **module-starter --module=Calibrate**
--author="*Your Name*" --email="*Your Email Address*"
– *this creates a folder named "Calibrate" containing module template files*

3 Open the **Calibrate/lib/Calibrate.pm** generated file and replace all the template code with that in the previous **MyModules/Calibrate.pm** package file

4 Still in **Calibrate/lib/Calibrate.pm**, add code under the usual **use** pragmas to identify the module's purpose and version number, then save the file
=head1 NAME
Calibrate - Temperature Conversion Utility.
=cut
our $VERSION = '1.0' ;

The name and version are used when building the module.

5 Next, open **Calibrate/t/00-load.t** in a text editor and replace the template code with the following testing code
```
#!perl
use strict ;
use warnings ;
use Test::More tests => 2 ;
use Calibrate qw(F2C C2F);
ok(F2C(32) == 0, "F2C function works") ;
ok(C2F(0) == 32, "C2F function works") ;
```

6 Save the testing file, then switch to the module folder and run the tests
Scripts> **cd Calibrate**
Scripts\Calibrate> **prove -I t**
– *this should produce a PASS result.*

7 Generate a "Makefile" with which to build the module
Scripts\Calibrate> **perl Makefile.PL**
– *this will generate a Makefile for Calibrate*

8 Then, build the module
Scripts\Calibrate> **make**
– *this triggers the building system to prepare the module file*

9 Now, test that the build was successful
Scripts\Calibrate> **make test**
– *this should produce a PASS result*

10 Finally, create a tarball archive for distribution
Scripts\Calibrate> **make dist**
- *this generates a tarball archive file, in this case named "Calibrate–1.0.tar.gz"*

Installation

The module can then be installed within the Perl environment to make it readily available alongside the standard modules.

1 Extract the contents of the tarball archive
Scripts\Calibrate> **tar zxf Calibrate-1.0.tar.gz**

2 Then, install the module on your system
Scripts\Calibrate> **make install**

3 Finally, test that the installation was successful
Scripts\Calibrate> **perl -MCalibrate -e "print \"All OK\";"**

You must observe character case for the **Makefile.PL** file name.

If the **gzip** compressor is not installed on your system, you can use an alternative such as **7-Zip**.

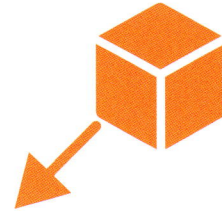

89

```
C:\Scripts\Calibrate>tar zxf Calibrate-1.0.tar.gz

C:\Scripts\Calibrate>make install
Installing C:\perl\site\lib\Calibrate.pm
Appending installation info to C:\perl\lib\perllocal.pod

C:\Scripts\Calibrate>perl -MCalibrate -e "print \"All OK\";"
All OK
```

Employing modules

The custom module on page 89 is installed in Perl's directory folder at **perl/site/lib**. As this is one of the locations that Perl automatically looks in to find modules, the custom module can easily be used in any Perl program.

temperature.pl

1 Begin a Perl program by specifying the custom module's name and function names

```perl
use strict ;
use warnings ;
use Calibrate qw(F2C C2F) ;
```

The built-in Perl **defined** function returns true only if the variable is indeed defined.

2 Add a subroutine function to test that an argument is a numeric value, including decimal and negative numbers

```perl
sub is_valid {
    my ( $temp ) = @_ ;
    return defined $temp && $temp =~ /^-?\d+(\.\d+)?$/ ;
}
```

3 Next, output a program heading

```perl
print "\nTEMPERATURE CONVERTER\n" ;
print "Fahrenheit-> Celsius (F) | " ;
print "Celsius-> Fahrenheit (C) \n".'-' x 51 ;
```

4 Now, begin a loop that requests user input and ensures it is uppercase

```perl
while (1) {
    print "\nSelect an option F, C, or Q to Quit: " ;
    chomp ( my $input = <STDIN> ) ;
    $input = uc( $input ) ;

    # Conditional test to be inserted here (Step 5).
}
```

This is a "forever loop" that will run indefinitely while true, until broken out by the **last** keyword.

5 Insert a conditional test that requests further user input

```perl
if ( $input =~ /^[FC]$/ ) {
    print "Enter " . ($input eq 'C' ? "Celsius: " : "Fahrenheit: ") ;
    chomp( my $temp = <STDIN> ) ;

    # Conditional test to be inserted here (Step 6).
}
elsif ( $input eq 'Q' ) {
    print "Goodbye!\n" ;
    last;
}
else { print "Invalid: Select F, C, or Q.\n"; }
```

The /^[FC]$/ regular expression allows only input of 'F' or 'C'.

6 Insert a conditional test to output results returned by functions in the custom module, or an error message

```perl
if ( is_valid( $temp ) ) {
    printf "%s %s is %.1f %s\n", $temp,
    ($input eq 'C' ? "Celsius" : "Fahrenheit"),
    ($input eq 'C' ? C2F($temp) : F2C($temp) ),
    ($input eq 'C' ? "Fahrenheit" : "Celsius");
}
else { print "Invalid: Must be a numeric value!\n"; }
```

7 Save the file then run the program and enter values to see the returned output

```
Command Prompt  ×  + ∨                          —   □   ×

C:\Scripts>perl temperature.pl

TEMPERATURE CONVERTER
Fahrenheit→ Celsius (F) | Celsius→ Fahrenheit (C)
─────────────────────────────────────────────
Select an option F, C, or Q to Quit: f
Enter Fahrenheit: 98.6
98.6 Fahrenheit is 37.0 Celsius

Select an option F, C, or Q to Quit: C
Enter Celsius: 37
37 Celsius is 98.6 Fahrenheit

Select an option F, C, or Q to Quit: F
Enter Fahrenheit: 72
72 Fahrenheit is 22.2 Celsius

Select an option F, C, or Q to Quit: X
Invalid: Select F, C, or Q.

Select an option F, C, or Q to Quit: c
Enter Celsius: xyz
Invalid: Must be a numeric value!

Select an option F, C, or Q to Quit: c
Enter Celsius: 22.2
22.2 Celsius is 72.0 Fahrenheit

Select an option F, C, or Q to Quit: C
Enter Celsius: -5.8
-5.8 Celsius is 21.6 Fahrenheit

Select an option F, C, or Q to Quit: Q
Goodbye!

C:\Scripts>
```

Summary

- A Perl subroutine function has the **sub** keyword followed by a valid name and **{ }** braces containing statements to execute.

- A subroutine function call specifies the function name followed by **( )** parentheses.

- Variables created outside functions have global scope.

- Variables created inside functions have local scope.

- Variables are initialized each time the function gets called unless made to persist with the special **state** keyword.

- Argument values can be passed to a subroutine function as a comma-separated list within the caller's **( )** parentheses.

- Arguments passed to a subroutine are assigned to an **@_** parameter array and can be referenced by their index number.

- The Perl **return** keyword can be included in the body of a subroutine function body to send values back to the caller.

- When passing a list to a subroutine, it must be the final argument to maintain the order of the list items.

- When passing a hash to a subroutine, Perl will flatten the key-value pairs into a sequential list without associations.

- Passing a hash reference to a subroutine places the memory address in the first element of the **@_** parameter array.

- Custom subroutine functions can be packaged inside a unique namespace to prevent variable and function name conflicts.

- A Perl package begins with the Perl **package** keyword followed by a name, and must end with a **1** statement.

- A Perl module is a reusable component that can contain one or more packages.

- Package function symbols can be imported into a script's namespace, so they may be referenced without a prefix.

- Custom Perl modules can be packaged as compressed tarball archives for sharing and deployment.

6 Reading and Writing Files

This chapter describes and demonstrates how to read and write text files using built-in Perl functions.

Creating directories

The technique for managing directories with Perl script consists of these three sequential parts:

- **Open** – a built-in Perl **opendir** function retrieves a reference to a directory (a "directory handle") and opens it for access.

- **Operation** – the built-in Perl functions listed in the table below can be used to perform various directory operations.

- **Close** – a built-in Perl **closedir** function releases the directory handle and closes the directory so that it is no longer accessible.

Function	Operation
readdir	Returns all file names and sub-directory names one-by-one.
rewinddir	Resets the position of the directory pointer to the beginning of the directory.
telldir	Returns the current position of the directory pointer while reading its entries.
seekdir	Resets the position of the directory pointer to a specified position within the directory.

It is useful to check if a directory already exists using a **-d** "file test operator". This returns true if a specified directory exists, otherwise it returns false. If a specified directory does not currently exist, it can be created using the built-in Perl **mkdir** function. This requires a directory name as its argument, and optionally a second argument to specify access permissions as an octal number.

To open a directory, the **opendir** function must assign the directory handle reference to a scalar variable (**$dh** by convention), and specify the name of a directory. To allow for errors, it is recommended to append an **or die** statement to terminate the program. This can output a special **$!** variable that contains an error message. The syntax to open a directory looks like this:

opendir $dh, q(*directory-name*) or die "Error: $!"

Operations can then be performed on the open directory, then it must always be closed by specifying the file handle as the argument to the **closedir** function.

Beware

Perl's **mkdir** function cannot automatically create sub-directories. It is necessary to first change into a parent directory using the Perl **chdir** function before calling the **mkdir** function.

1 Begin a Perl program by initializing a scalar variable with the name of a directory

```perl
use strict ;
use warnings ;
my $dir = 'Data' ;
```

directory.pl

2 Next, create a new directory if not already existing and specify access permissions for the directory

```perl
unless ( -d $dir ) {
    mkdir $dir, 0744 or die "Error: $!" ;
    print "Directory '$dir' created successfully.\n" ;
    print "Owner can modify, others can read.\n" ;
}
else { print "Directory '$dir' already exists.\n" ; }
```

3 Now, attempt to open the directory

```perl
opendir my $dh, $dir or die "Error: $!" ;
```

4 Then, list all files within the directory

```perl
while (my $file = readdir($dh) ) { print "File: $file \n" ; }
```

5 Finally, remember to close the open directory, or terminate the program

```perl
closedir $dh ;
```

6 Save the file, then run the program twice to see the confirmation message and its default directory contents

```
Command Prompt    X    +    v                      —    □    ×

C:\Scripts>perl directory.pl
Directory 'Data' created successfully.
Owner can modify, others can read.
File: .
File: ..

C:\Scripts>perl directory.pl
Directory 'Data' already exists.
File: .
File: ..
```

Hot tip

The **Data** directory created here will be used in ensuing examples to store text files.

Writing files

The technique for handling file content with Perl script consists of these three sequential parts:

- **Open** – a built-in Perl **open** function retrieves a reference to a file (a "file handle") and opens the file for access.

- **Action** – a "mode" specifier determines how the file content can be treated while the file is accessible in its open state.

- **Close** – a built-in Perl **close** function releases the file handle and closes the file so that it is no longer accessible.

The possible file modes are listed in the following table:

Mode	Action
<	Read-only
>	Write (deletes all existing content)
>>	Append (adds to existing content)
+<	Read and Write
+>	Write and Read (deletes all existing content)
+>>	Read and Append (adds to existing content)

Don't forget

Although the **>** write mode can create a new file if none exists, it cannot create a new directory.

To open a file, the **open** function must assign the file handle reference to a scalar variable (**$fh** by convention), specify the **>** write file mode, and specify the name of a file. If a file of the specified name does not exist, a new file of that name will be created. Access permissions can optionally be specified using the **chmod** function. To allow for possible errors, an **or die** statement can output the **$!** variable error message. The syntax to open a file for writing might, therefore, look something like this:

```
open my $fh, q(>), q(file-name) or die "Error: $!"
```

Content can then be written to the open file simply by having the **print** function output to the file handle. After reading, writing, or appending to a file it must always be closed by specifying the file handle as the argument to the **close** function.

1 Begin a Perl program by initializing variables with a directory name, a file name, and some text content

```perl
use strict ;
use warnings ;
my ( $dir, $file ) = ( 'Data', 'spite.txt' ) ;
my $str = "\nIt would be spiteful
To put jellyfish in a trifle.\n" ;
```

write.pl

2 Next, open the file for writing and set access permissions

```perl
open my $fh, q(>), "$dir/$file" or die "Error: $!" ;
chmod 0744, $file ;
```

3 Now, write the text content into the file, line-by-line

```perl
print $fh $str ;
```

Hot tip

4 Then, close the open file, or terminate the program

```perl
close $fh or die "Error: $!" ;
```

Notice that the file is written a line at a time.

5 Finally, output confirmation of writing success

```perl
print "\nFile: $file written successfully.\n" ;
print "Owner can modify, others can read.\n" ;
```

6 Save the file, then run the program to see the confirmation message

```
Command Prompt          +  ˅                    —  □  ×

C:\Scripts>perl write.pl

File: spite.txt written successfully.
Owner can modify, others can read.

C:\Scripts>type Data\spite.txt

It would be spiteful
To put jellyfish in a trifle.
```

7 Use the **type** command on Windows, or the **cat** command on Linux, to see the new file's content in the Terminal

Appending text

To open a file to add to existing content the **open** function must assign the file handle reference to a scalar variable, specify the **>>** append file mode, and specify the name of a file. If a file of the specified name does not exist, a new file of that name will be created. The syntax to open a file to append might look like this:

open my $file_handle, q(>>), q(*file-name*) or die "Error: $!"

Content can now be appended to the open file by having the **print** function output to the file handle, then the file can be closed.

append.pl

1 Begin a Perl program by initializing variables with a directory name, a file name, and a text attribution
```
use strict ;
use warnings ;
my ( $dir, $file ) = ( 'Data', 'spite.txt' ) ;
my $attrib = "– Karl \n" ;
```

2 Next, open the file for appending
```
open my $fh, q(>>), "$dir/$file" or die "Error: $!" ;
```

3 Now, write the text content into the file, line by line
```
print $fh $attrib ;
```

4 Then, close the open file or terminate the program
```
close $fh or die "Error: $!" ;
```

5 Finally, output a confirmation of writing success
```
print "\nAttribution: $attrib appended to $file.\n" ;
```

6 Save the file, then run the program to see the confirmation message

```
C:\Scripts>perl append.pl

Attribution: – Karl
 appended to spite.txt.

C:\Scripts>_
```

Reading files

To open a file to read existing content the **open** function must assign the file handle reference to a scalar variable, specify the **<** read file mode, and specify the name of a file. If a file of the specified name does not exist, an error will be created. The syntax to open a file to read might look like this:

```
open my $file_handle, q(<), q(file-name) or die "Error: $!"
```

Content can then be read from the open file by a loop that passes each line of content in turn from a **<$file_handle>** placeholder to the **print** function for output, then the file can be closed.

1 Begin a Perl program by initializing variables with a directory name and a file name
```
use strict ;
use warnings ;
my ( $dir, $file ) = ( 'Data', 'spite.txt' ) ;
```

2 Next, open the file for reading
```
open my $fh, q(<), "$dir/$file" or die "Error: $!" ;
```

3 Now, read the text content from the file, line by line
```
while (my $line = <$fh> )
    print $line ;
}
```

4 Then, close the open file or terminate the program
```
close $fh or die "Error: $!" ;
```

5 Save the file, then run the program to see output read from the file

read.pl

```
C:\Scripts>perl read.pl

It would be spiteful
To put jellyfish in a trifle.
- Karl
```

Writing & reading

The Perl **+>** mode will open (or create and open) a file and remove any existing content. In this mode, content can be written into the file. The file pointer can then be reset to the beginning of the file by the Perl **seek** function so that all content can be read.

PL

write_read.pl

1 Begin a Perl program by including the **DateTime** module and initialize variables with a directory name and a file name
```
use strict ;
use warnings ;
use DateTime ;
my ( $dir, $file ) = ( 'Data', 'edition.txt' ) ;
```

2 Next, open a file in write-read mode
```
open my $fh, q(+>), "$dir/$file" or die "Error: $!" ;
```

3 Now, write a string containing the current time into the file and output the current time
```
my $dt = DateTime->now ;
my $time = $dt->hms ;
print $fh 'Entry created at: '.$time ;
print "Written to file at $time\n" ;
```

4 Then, read and output all content from the file
```
seek( $fh, 0, 0 ) ;
while ( my $line = <$fh> ) {
    print "Read from file:\t$line\n" ;
}
```

5 Finally, close the file
```
close $fh or die "Error: $!" ;
```

6 Save the file, then run the program twice to see the written content read and output

Hot tip

The arguments to the **seek** function specify the file handle, the offset to move the pointer by (**0** means no movement), and the pointer position (**0** means start of file).

```
Command Prompt

C:\Scripts>perl write_read.pl
Written to file at 08:49:43
Read from file: Entry created at: 08:49:43

C:\Scripts>perl write_read.pl
Written to file at 08:52:26
Read from file: Entry created at: 08:52:26
```

100

Reading & writing

The Perl **+>** mode will open (or create and open) a file and remove any existing content. In this mode, content can be written into the file. The file pointer can then be reset to the beginning of the file by the Perl **seek** function so that all content can be read.

1 Begin a Perl program by including the **DateTime** module and initialize variables with a directory name and a file name

```perl
use strict ;
use warnings ;
my ( $dir, $file ) = ( 'Data', 'version.txt' ) ;
```

2 Next, create a file if not existing and add some content

```perl
unless ( -e $dir.'/'.$file ) {
    open my $fh, q(>), "$dir/$file" or die "Error: $!" ;
    print $fh 'Version #1' ;
    close $fh or die "Error: $!" ;
}
```

3 Now, open a file in read-write mode and read all content

```perl
open my $fh, q(+<), "$dir/$file" or die "Error: $!" ;
my $line = <$fh> ;
print "Read from file: \t$line" ;
```

4 Then, write and output all content from the file

```perl
$line = ($line eq 'Version #1') ? 'Version #2' : 'Version #1' ;
seek( $fh, 0, 0 ) ;
print $fh $line ;
print "\nWritten to file:\t$line\n" ;
```

5 Finally, close the file

```perl
close $fh or die "Error: $!" ;
```

6 Save the file, then run the program three times to see the content read and written in output

PL

read_write.pl

```
Command Prompt    ✕    +  ✕                      —  □  ✕

C:\Scripts>perl read_write.pl
Read from file:          Version #1
Written to file:         Version #2

C:\Scripts>perl read_write.pl
Read from file:          Version #2
Written to file:         Version #1
```

Reading & appending

The Perl **+>>** mode will open (or create and open) a file and retain any existing content. In this mode, content can be appended to the file. The file pointer can then be reset to the beginning of the file by the Perl **seek** function so that all content can be read:

read_append.pl

1 Begin a Perl program by including the **DateTime** module and variables with a directory name, a file name, and the time

```perl
use strict ;
use warnings ;
use DateTime ;
my ( $dir, $file ) = ( 'Data', 'message.txt' ) ;
my $time = DateTime->now->hms ;
```

2 Next, create or open a file in which to read and append

```perl
open my $fh, q(+>>), "$dir/$file" or die "Error: $!" ;
```

3 Now, if the file is empty, append three lines (a message header, a message body, and a message timestamp) then output a confirmation and exit the program

```perl
if ( -z "$dir/$file" ) {
    print $fh "Message #1" ;
    print $fh "\nWelcome to Perl messages." ;
    print $fh "\nCreated at $time\n" ;
    close $fh or die "Error: $!" ;
    print "New $dir file '$file' created.\n" ;
    exit ;
}
```

The file test operator **-z** returns true if the file exists but has zero bytes.

4 Then, for an existing file, read all content and output the message body in the second line of the final message

```perl
seek( $fh, 0, 0 ) ;
my @lines = <$fh> ;
my $msg = $lines[-2] ;
print "Read from file:\t $msg" ;
```

5 Next, read the message number from the message header in the first line of the final message

```perl
my $hdr = $lines[-3] ;
chomp $hdr ;
my $num = chop($hdr) ;
```

The **chomp** function removes a newline, if there is one, and the **chop** function removes and returns the final character in a string.

6 Append a new header with the next number

```perl
$num++ ;
print $fh "Message # $num \n" ;
```

7 Append a new message body, simulated by a random hexadecimal number
```perl
printf $fh "%08X\n", rand(0xFFFFFFFF) ;
```

8 Append a current message timestamp
```perl
print $fh "Updated at $time...\n" ;
```

9 Finally, close the file
```perl
close $fh or die "Error: $!" ;
```

10 Save the file then run the program several times to see the content read and appended in output

```
Command Prompt     ×    +  ⌄                            —    □    ×

C:\Scripts>perl read_append.pl
New Data file 'message.txt' created.

C:\Scripts>perl read_append.pl
Read from file: Welcome to Perl messages.

C:\Scripts>perl read_append.pl
Read from file: BD93870D

C:\Scripts>perl read_append.pl
Read from file: 0689300C
```

```
message.txt            ×    +                  —    □    ×
File    Edit    View

Message #1
Welcome to Perl messages.
Created at 11:53:41

Message #2
BD93870D
Updated at 11:54:11 ...

Message #3
0689300C
Updated at 11:55:16 ...

Message #4
98171C99
Updated at 11:56:16 ...
```

Hot tip

The **rand** function returns a random number between 0 and the number specified by its argument.

Summary

- The **opendir** function opens a directory, to allow operations within the directory, and **closedir** closes the directory.

- The **opendir** function assigns a directory handle to a variable – named **$dh** by convention – and specifies a directory name.

- The **-d** file test operator returns true if a specified directory exists, otherwise it returns false.

- The **readdir** function returns all file names and sub-directory names within an open directory.

- The directory pointer in an open directory can be controlled by the **rewinddir**, **telldir**, and **seekdir** functions.

- The **open** function opens a file to allow mode operations within the file, and the **close** function closes the file.

- The **>** mode allows content to be written in an open file.

- The **<** mode allows content to be read from an open file.

- The **>>** mode allows content to be appended to an open file.

- The **+>** mode allows both writing and reading in an open file.

- The **+<** mode allows both reading and writing in an open file.

- The **+>>** mode allows reading and appending in an open file.

- The **>** write mode and the **+>** write and read mode will both delete all existing content when the file opens.

- The **open** function assigns a file handle to a variable – named **$fh** by convention – then specifies a file mode and file name.

- An **or die** statement will terminate a program and can output a special **$!** variable that contains an error message.

- The file pointer can be reset to the beginning of a file by the **seek** function so that all content can be read.

- The **-z** file test operator returns true if a specified file exists and is empty, otherwise it returns false.

7 Programming with Objects

Creating classes

Object-Oriented Programming (OOP) attempts to represent real-life objects that have properties and behaviors. For example, each car has a color property and an acceleration behavior.

In Perl, an object is created from a Perl package whose name defines a class name. The class package contains a "constructor" subroutine to define the class with attributes (properties) and methods (behaviors). Typically, a constructor is named "new".

A constructor first receives the class name and passed argument values in the special @_ array. It next creates a $self hash reference to store the argument values. A built-in Perl **bless** function then associates the hash reference with the class, so the hash values become attributes of the class. Finally, the constructor returns the object to the caller. A constructor therefore looks like this:

```
sub new {
   my ($class, $argument-name) = @_ ;
   my $self = { attribute-name => $argument-name } ;
   bless $self, $class ;
   return $self ;
}
```

Following the class constructor, the package can define a "getter" subroutine to retrieve an attribute from the class. This begins by extracting the first element of $self using the Perl **shift** function, which is a reference to the class hash. The hash reference can then be used to access the object attributes. So, a getter has this syntax:

```
sub getter-name {
   $self = shift ;
   return $self->{attribute-name} ;
}
```

In a simple program it is common to create a package named "main" in which to create objects and to execute their methods.

An object is created by calling the class constructor, passing arguments to become attributes, and assigning the returned object to a scalar variable – whose name is the object name. The getter method can then be called to retrieve an attribute of that object:

```
package main ;

my $object-name ;

print $object-name->getter-name( ) ;
```

...cont'd

The Perl built-in **ref** function can be used to examine whether its argument is a reference. If so, this returns the type of reference or the class name if the reference is blessed inside an object.

1 Begin a Perl package for a class named "Person"
```perl
package Person ;
use strict ;
use warnings ;
```

2 Next, add a constructor subroutine function
```perl
sub new {
    my ($class, $name) = @_ ;
    my $self = { name => $name } ;
    bless $self, $class ;
    return $self ;
}
```

3 Now, add a getter subroutine function
```perl
sub speak {
    my $self = shift ;
    return "\nHello, I'm " . $self->{name} . "!\n" ;
}
```

4 Then, begin a new package for execution statements
```perl
package main ;
use strict ;
use warnings ;
```

5 Create an object (instance) of the **Person** class
```perl
my $author = Person->new( "Mike McGrath" ) ;
print ref($author) ? ref($author) . " created." : "Error." ;
```

6 Finally, call the getter function of the object
```perl
print $author->speak( ) ;
```

7 Save the file then run the program to see the object created and its behavior executed

PL
class.pl

```
C:\Scripts>perl class.pl
Person created.
Hello, I'm Mike McGrath!
```

Creating objects

Multiple objects, each having multiple attributes, can be created as individual instances of a single class. The constructor can check that it has received the correct number of arguments and can provide default attribute values using the || OR operator. This will use the default value for an attribute if the constructor receives an empty string, **0**, or the keyword **undef** as any argument.

In addition to getter methods, to retrieve the attributes, the class may also define "setter" methods to update the attributes with new values. These receive the class and argument values from the caller, and assign the argument values to attributes of the class object.

object.pl

1 Begin a Perl package for a class named "Dog"

```perl
package Dog ;
use strict ;
use warnings ;
```

2 Next, add a constructor subroutine function that checks it has received enough arguments and provides defaults

```perl
sub new {
    my ($class, $name, $color, $age) = @_ ;
    die "\n$_[0] constructor needs 3 values!\n" if @_ != 4 ;
    my $self = {
        name  => $name  || 'unknown',
        color => $color || 'black',
        age   => $age   || 1
    } ;
    bless $self, $class ;
    return $self ;
}
```

3 Now, add getter methods

```perl
sub get_color {
    my $self = shift ;
    return $self->{color} ;
}

sub get_age {
    my $self = shift ;
    return $self->{age} ;
}
```

...cont'd

4 Then, add setter methods

```perl
sub set_color {
    my ($self, $color) = @_ ;
    $self->{color} = $color ;
}

sub set_age {
    my ($self, $age) = @_ ;
    $self->{age} = $age ;
}
```

5 Finally, add a method to describe the object

```perl
sub describe {
    my $self = shift ;
    return printf "%s is a %s dog aged %d years.\n",
        $self->{name}, $self->{color}, $self->{age} ;
}
```

6 Then, begin a new package for execution statements

```perl
package main ;
use strict ;
use warnings ;
```

7 Next, create and describe two objects of the **Dog** class

```perl
my $fido = Dog->new( 'Fido', 'brown', 3 ) ;
my $coco = Dog->new( 'Coco', undef, 0 ) ;
$fido->describe( ) ;
$coco->describe( ) ;
```

8 Now, update and describe one object

```perl
print "\nSome years later...\n" ;
$fido->set_color( 'gray' ) ;
$fido->set_age( 10 ) ;
$fido->describe( ) ;
```

9 Save the file then run the program to see the objects

```
C:\Scripts>perl object.pl
Fido is a brown dog aged 3 years.
Coco is a black dog aged 2 years.

Some years later...
Fido is a gray dog aged 10 years.
```

Notice that two undefined arguments are replaced with default values. Remove these completely and run the program again to see it terminated by the **die** statement.

109

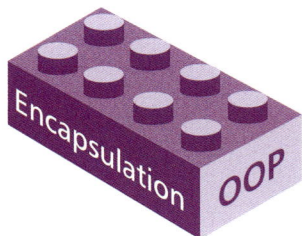

Encapsulating data

The three cornerstones of Object-Oriented Programming are: **Encapsulation**, Inheritance, and Polymorphism.

Encapsulation encloses data within classes to restrict direct access to the data – the data should only be accessible via methods. In the previous example, the data is stored in a hash reference (**$self**) that can be accessed by getter methods, but is also directly accessible – for example, with **$fido->{color}**.

In order to enforce encapsulation in Perl, lexical variables that have only local scope can be used to make the data private, and anonymous subroutines ("closures") can control access.

Anonymous subroutines are functions that do not have a name. They can be assigned to a variable so that the variable stores a reference to the anonymous subroutine. The syntax **->( )** can then be appended after the variable name to call the subroutine:

```
my $data = "Hello!\n" ;
my $anon = sub { print $data } ;
$anon->( ) ;                            # Outputs Hello!
```

A constructor can store a reference in the object's hash to an anonymous subroutine, and the **->( )** syntax can be appended to that in order to call the anonymous subroutine:

```
$self->{call_anon} = sub { print $data } ;

$object-name->{call_anon}->( ) ;       # Outputs Hello!
```

It is, however, recommended to create a class method to implement the call to improve readability and flexibility:

```
sub get_data {
   my ($self) = @_ ;
   $self->{call_anon}->( ) ;
}
```

This now allows the anonymous subroutine to be called, like this:

```
$object-name->get_data( ) ;            # Outputs Hello!
```

The reference to the anonymous subroutine (**call_anon**) is a visible part of the data structure, but the variable (**$data**) is completely encapsulated and is not directly accessible.

...cont'd

1 Begin a Perl package for a class named "Private"

```perl
package Private ;
use strict ;
use warnings ;
```

2 Next, add a constructor subroutine that initializes variables with local scope and assigns anonymous subroutines to object references

```perl
sub new {
    my ($class) = @_ ;
    my $data = "\n1. Private Data\n" ;
    my $self = bless { }, $class ;
    $self->{return_data} = sub { return $data } ;
    $self->{update_data} = sub {$data = shift } ;
    return $self ;
}
```

3 Add getter and setter methods to call the anonymous subroutines

```perl
sub get_data {
    my ($self) = @_ ;
    return $self->{return_data}->( ) ;
}

sub set_data {
    my ($self, $str) = @_ ;
    return $self->{update_data}->($str) ;
}
```

4 Now, create an object (class instance) and call its methods

```perl
my $obj = Private->new( ) ;
print $obj->get_data( ) ;

$obj->set_data( "2. New Private Data\n" ) ;
print $obj->get_data( ) ;
```

5 Save the file then run the program to see encapsulation

```
C:\Scripts>perl encap.pl

1. Private Data
2. New Private Data
```

encap.pl

Hot tip

The **bless { }** statement creates an anonymous hash – a new empty hash is allocated in the memory.

Hot tip

Perl provides a **Data::Dumper** module that can be used to inspect data structures. Add **use Data::Dumper;** and **print Dumper($obj);** to see visible object components.

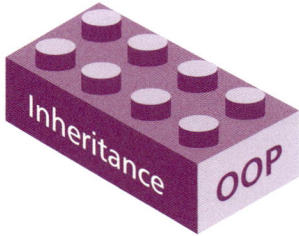

Inheriting features

The three cornerstones of Object-Oriented Programming are: Encapsulation, **Inheritance**, and Polymorphism.

Inheritance is the ability of attributes and methods of a parent class to be available in child classes. This avoids the need to repeat the same code in each class.

Perl provides a special **@ISA** array that lists parent classes. When a method is called, Perl first looks for it in the object class. If the method isn't found there, Perl then looks for it in the **@ISA** array. This allows the child class to execute the method created in the parent class. Alternatively, a child class method of the same name will override that in the parent class.

PL

inherit.pl

1 Begin a Perl package for a class named "Parent"
```perl
package Parent ;
use strict ;
use warnings ;
```

2 Next, add a constructor method and a custom method
```perl
sub new {
    my ($class, $name, $hair_color) = @_ ;
    my $self = {
        name => $name,
        hair_color => $hair_color
        } ;
    bless $self, $class ;
    return $self ;
}

sub greet {
    my ($self) = @_ ;
    return "I am $self->{name} ".
    "and I have $self->{hair_color} hair.\n" ;
}
```

Don't forget

This statement requires the **our** scope to declare a global variable and the **qw** function to assign a list type to the array – using the **q** function would be incorrect as it returns a single string.

3 Add a child class that will inherit the custom method from its parent class
```perl
package Son ;
use strict ;
use warnings ;
our @ISA = qw(Parent) ;
```

112

...cont'd

4 Now, add a child class that will inherit from its parent class and override the custom method in its parent class

```perl
package Daughter ;
use strict ;
use warnings ;
our @ISA = qw(Parent) ;

sub greet {
    my ($self) = @_ ;
    return "I'm $self->{name} and I inherited ".
    "$self->{hair_color} hair from my parent!\n" ;
}
```

5 Then, begin a new package for execution statements

```perl
package main ;
use strict ;
use warnings ;
```

6 Finally, create three objects and call their method

```perl
my $parent = Parent->new( "Barbara", "Black" ) ;
print $parent->greet( ) ;

my $son = Son->new( "Michael", "Brown" ) ;
print $son->greet( ) ;

my $daughter = Daughter->new(
        "Susan", $parent->{hair_color} ) ;
print $daughter->greet( ) ;
```

7 Save the file then run the program to see output from the inherited method and attribute

```
C:\Scripts>perl inherit.pl

I am Barbara and I have Black hair.

I am Michael and I have Brown hair.

I'm Susan and I inherited Black hair from my parent!
```

The term "ISA" is not an acronym, but can be thought of as meaning "IS A descendant".

Alternatively, you can replace the **@ISA** array statements with a **use parent** pragma if the parent class is defined in a separate module file. In this case, with the **Parent** class defined in a file named **Parent.pm**, the **our @ISA qw(Parent)** statements could be replaced by **use parent qw(Parent)** statements.

113

Exploiting diversity

The three cornerstones of Object-Oriented Programming are: Encapsulation, Inheritance, and **Polymorphism**.

Polymorphism (from Greek, meaning "many forms") is the ability to assign a different meaning or purpose to an entity according to its context.

In Perl, polymorphism allows objects of different classes to be treated as instances of a common parent class. Different classes can define their own version of a method by overriding a parent class method to respond to a method call in different ways.

poly.pl

1 Begin a Perl package for a class named "Bird"
```perl
package Bird ;
use strict ;
use warnings ;
```

2 Next, add a constructor method and two custom methods
```perl
sub new {
    my ($class, $sound) = @_ ;
    my $self = { sound => $sound } ;
    bless $self, $class ;
    return $self ;
}

sub talk {
    my ($self) = @_ ;
    print "\n"."$self->{sound}! " x 2 ;
}

sub fly {
    print "\nA bird takes flight!\n" ;
}
```

3 Add a child class that will inherit the custom methods from its parent class and override one as its own version
```perl
package Pigeon ;
use strict ;
use warnings ;
our @ISA = qw(Bird) ;
sub fly  {
    print "\nA pigeon flies away...\n" ;
}
```

4 Add another child class that will also inherit the custom methods and override one as its own version

```perl
package Chicken ;
use strict ;
use warnings ;
our @ISA = qw(Bird) ;
sub fly  {
    print "\nI'm just a chicken - I can't fly!\n" ;
}
```

5 Add a further child class that will simply inherit the custom methods from its parent class

```perl
package Owl ;
use strict ;
use warnings ;
our @ISA = qw(Bird) ;
```

6 Then, begin a new package for execution statements

```perl
package main ;
use strict ;
use warnings ;
```

7 Finally, create three objects and call their methods

```perl
my $pigeon  = Pigeon->new( 'Coo' ) ;
my $chicken = Chicken->new( 'Cluck' ) ;
my $owl = Owl->new( 'Hoot' ) ;

foreach my $bird ($pigeon, $chicken, $owl) {
    $bird->talk( ), $bird->fly( ) ;
}
```

8 Save the file then run the program to see diverse output from the same method calls

```
Command Prompt  X    +  v                  —   □   X

C:\Scripts>perl poly.pl

Coo! Coo!
A pigeon flies away...

Cluck! Cluck!
I'm just a chicken — I can't fly!

Hoot! Hoot!
A bird takes flight!
```

Don't forget

It is considered best practice to include the **use strict** and **use warnings** statements in every package to ensure that errors are identified at their source.

115

Summary

- Object-Oriented Programming (OOP) attempts to represent the properties and behaviors of real-life objects.

- An object is created from a Perl package whose name defines a class name.

- A constructor defines class attributes and methods.

- The class name and arguments passed to a constructor by the caller are received by the @_ array.

- Arguments passed to a class can be copied into a $self hash reference to become attributes of the class object.

- The bless function associates a $self hash reference with the class.

- The constructor finally returns the class object to the caller.

- The first element of $self is a reference to the class hash, and can be extracted using the Perl shift function.

- An object attribute is accessed by dereferencing the hash reference using $self->{ attribute-name }.

- A caller can pass an undefined argument to a constructor as a 0 character as an empty string or as the undef keyword.

- Getter methods retrieve attributes of an object, and setter methods update object attribute values.

- The three cornerstones of Object-Oriented Programming are encapsulation, inheritance, and polymorphism.

- Encapsulation encloses data in classes to restrict direct access.

- Lexical variables with local scope can make data private, and anonymous subroutines can control access to the data.

- Anonymous subroutines can be assigned to a variable, and can be called by appending ->( ) after the variable name.

- Inheritance is the ability of attributes and methods of a parent class to be available in child classes.

- Polymorphism allows objects of different classes to be treated as instances of a common parent class.

8 Using Databases

SQLite database

Introducing databases

Databases are simply convenient storage containers that store data in a structured manner. Every database is composed of one or more tables that structure the data into organized rows and columns. This makes it easy to reference and manipulate the data.

Each database table column has a label to identify the data stored within the table cells in that column. Each row contains an entry called a "record" that places data in each cell along that row.

A typical simple database table looks like this:

```
+----------+------------+-----------+-----------------+
| user_id  | first_name | last_name | email           |
+----------+------------+-----------+-----------------+
|        1 | Mike       | McGrath   | mike@example.com |
|        2 | Susan      | Andrews   | sue@example.com  |
|        3 | Bob        | Williams  | bob@example.com  |
+----------+------------+-----------+-----------------+
```

The rows of a database table are not automatically arranged in any particular order, so they can be sorted alphabetically, numerically or by any other criteria. It is important, therefore, to have some means to identify each record in the table. The example above allocates a "user_id" for this purpose, and this unique identifier is known as the **PRIMARY KEY**.

Storing data in a single table is very useful, but relational databases with multiple tables introduce more possibilities by allowing the stored data to be combined in a variety of ways. For instance, the following two tables could be added to the database containing the first example table shown above:

Hot tip

The column labels "user_id" and "book_id" include an underscore character because spaces are not allowed in labels.

```
+---------+-----------------+        +---------+---------+
| book_id | title           |        | user_id | book_id |
+---------+-----------------+        +---------+---------+
|       1 | Don Quixote     |        |       1 |       2 |
|       2 | The Great Gatsby |       |       2 |       1 |
|       3 | Moby Dick       |        |       3 |       3 |
+---------+-----------------+        +---------+---------+
```

The table on the left lists several book titles sorted numerically by "book_id" number. The table on the right describes a relationship between the tables that links each user to the book they have borrowed. So...

Mike McGrath (user #1) borrowed The Great Gatsby (book #2), Susan Andrews (user #2) borrowed Don Quixote (book #1), and Bob Williams (user #3) borrowed Moby Dick (book #3).

Connecting a database

The Strawberry Perl installation on Windows includes the popular SQLite server-less, lightweight database engine. This operates from a file, making it ideal for embedded apps and local storage.

The Perl **DBI** (DataBase Interface) module is used to connect to the SQLite engine. Its **connect** method requires a string argument to specify a driver (SQLite) and a database name to acquire a database handle, user name, and password (or empty strings), and instructions to raise errors upon failure. Queries may then be made to manipulate the database, and the connection closed by calling the connection's **disconnect** method.

Hot tip

If SQLite is not installed, users can install the required module with **cpan DBI** and **cpan DBD::SQLite** commands.

1 Begin a Perl script by including the **DBI** module
```
use strict ;
use warnings ;
use DBI ;
```

db-connect.pl

2 Next attempt to establish a database connection using the SQLite driver and a name of "library.db", or output an error string message from the database engine
```
my $dbh =
    DBI->connect( "dbi:SQLite:dbname=library.db",
    "", "", { RaiseError => 1 } )
    or die "Cannot connect: $DBI::errstr " ;
```

Hot tip

The **connect** method may specify optional username and password arguments, but are simply assigned empty strings here.

3 Now, output a message confirming success
```
print "\nConnected to DATABASE successfully!\n" ;
# SQL queries will be inserted here in further examples.
```

4 Finally, close the connection
```
$dbh->disconnect ;
```

5 Save and run the program to connect to a database

```
Command Prompt

C:\Scripts>perl db-connect.pl

Connected to DATABASE successfully!
```

```
mike@LinuxPC: ~/Scripts

mike@LinuxPC:~/Scripts$ perl db-connect.pl

Connected to DATABASE successfully!
```

Adding tables

Perl can interact with a database by building SQL (Structured Query Language) queries. The first requirement is to add a table to the database in which to deposit data. The SQL query for this begins with **CREATE TABLE IF NOT EXISTS** *table-name*. This statement is followed by parentheses containing a list of table row specifications. These allocate a row name and describe the type of data the row can contain. The query is assigned to a variable, and can be executed by specifying that variable name as the argument to the database handle's **do** method.

db-table.pl

1 Begin a Perl script by connecting to a database
```
use strict ; use warnings ; use DBI ;
my $dbh =
    DBI->connect( "dbi:SQLite:dbname=library.db",
    "", "", { RaiseError => 1 } )
    or die "Cannot connect: $DBI::errstr " ;
```

2 Next, build an SQL query for a table of three rows
```
my $sql = "CREATE TABLE IF NOT EXISTS users (
    id INTEGER PRIMARY KEY AUTOINCREMENT,
    name TEXT NOT NULL,
    email TEXT NOT NULL)" ;
```

3 Now, attempt to add the table to the database
```
$dbh->do($sql) ;
```

4 Now, output a message confirming success
```
print "\nTable 'users' added successfully!\n" ;
```

5 Finally, close the connection
```
$dbh->disconnect ;
```

6 Save and run the program to add the table

Hot tip

The **id** field will contain a unique reference number for each user. **AUTOINCREMENT** will automatically generate successive numbers. **NOT NULL** is a "constraint" that insists the **name** and **email** fields cannot be empty.

Hot tip

You can discover more on the Structured Query Language in the companion book SQL in easy steps.

```
C:\Scripts>perl db-table.pl

Table 'users' added successfully!
```

Explaining tables

The database handle's **do** method simply executes a given SQL query, but for more complex or repeated actions there are **prepare** and **execute** methods. The **prepare** method accepts an SQL query as its argument and returns a statement handle. This has an **execute** method that executes the query, and a **finish** method to ensure the query was fully executed.

To explain the structure of a table, its name can be specified as the argument to an SQLite **PRAGMA table_info()** function and the row details extracted from the statement handle's **fetchrow_array**.

1 Begin a Perl script by connecting to a database
```perl
use strict ; use warnings ; use DBI ;
my $dbh =
    DBI->connect( "dbi:SQLite:dbname=library.db",
    "", "", { RaiseError => 1 } )
    or die "Cannot connect: $DBI::errstr " ;
```

db-explain.pl

2 Next, assign table details to a statement handle
```perl
my $sth = $dbh->prepare( "PRAGMA table_info(users)" ) ;
$sth->execute( ) ;
```

3 Now, output the table headers, rows, and columns
```perl
printf "%-10s" x 6 . "\n",
    qw(col name type not_null default pk) ;
print "-" x 60, "\n";
while (my @row = $sth->fetchrow_array) {
    $_ //= " " for @row ;
    printf "%-10s" x 6 . "\n", @row ;
}
```

4 Finally, close the statement and database connection
```perl
$sth->finish( ) ;
$dbh->disconnect( ) ;
```

5 Save and run the program to see the table structure

```
Command Prompt  X    +  v                        —  □  ✕

C:\Scripts>perl db-explain.pl
col        name       type       not_null   default   pk

0          id         INTEGER    0                     1
1          name       TEXT       1                     0
2          email      TEXT       1                     0
```

Hot tip

In this table, the **col** column ID gets automatically numbered, and the user **id** is the primary key (**pk**). The **name** and **email** fields may not be left empty (**not_null**).

Listing tables

The "users" table created in the previous example sets its "id" column as its **PRIMARY KEY** to allow its data to be referenced from other tables. The process to create a relationship between tables requires a **FOREIGN KEY** in a second table to reference the **PRIMARY KEY** in the first table. The syntax looks like this:

> **FOREIGN KEY (***first-table-id***) REFERENCES** *first-table-name***(id)**

In addition to the "users" table, a "books" table could be created with an "id" column as its **PRIMARY KEY**. A "loans" table could then be added with **FOREIGN KEY** fields to reference both **PRIMARY KEY** fields in the "users" table and the "books" table:

db-foreign.pl

1 Begin a Perl script by connecting to a database
```perl
use strict ; use warnings ; use DBI ;
my $dbh =
    DBI->connect( "dbi:SQLite:dbname=library.db",
    "", "", { RaiseError => 1 } )
    or die "Cannot connect: $DBI::errstr " ;
```

2 Next, build an SQL query for a table of two rows
```perl
my $sql = "CREATE TABLE IF NOT EXISTS books (
    id INTEGER PRIMARY KEY AUTOINCREMENT,
    title TEXT NOT NULL)" ;
```

3 Now, attempt to add the table to the database
```perl
$dbh->do($sql) ;
print "\nTable 'books' added successfully!\n" ;
```

4 Then, build an SQL query for a table of three rows
```perl
$sql = "CREATE TABLE IF NOT EXISTS loans (
    id INTEGER PRIMARY KEY AUTOINCREMENT,
    user_id INTEGER NOT NULL,
    book_id INTEGER NOT NULL,
    FOREIGN KEY (user_id) REFERENCES users(id),
    FOREIGN KEY (book_id) REFERENCES books(id)
)" ;
```

5 Finally, attempt to add the table to the database
```perl
$dbh->do($sql) ;
print "\nTable 'loans' added successfully!\n" ;
$dbh->disconnect( ) ;
```

6 Save and run the program to add the tables

SQLite contains an internal system table named **sqlite_master** that stores information about the database itself. The SQL query **SELECT name FROM sqlite_master WHERE type='table'** can be used to list the names of all tables within the database.

1 Begin a Perl script by connecting to a database
```perl
use strict ; use warnings ; use DBI ;
my $dbh =
    DBI->connect( "dbi:SQLite:dbname=library.db",
    "", "", { RaiseError => 1 } )
    or die "Cannot connect: $DBI::errstr " ;
```

db-list.pl

2 Now, assign table details to a statement handle
```perl
my $sth = $dbh->prepare(
"SELECT name FROM sqlite_master WHERE type='table' " ) ;
$sth->execute( ) ;
```

3 Then, output a list of all table names
```perl
while (my ($table) = $sth->fetchrow_array) {
    print "Table: $table\n";
}
```

4 Finally, close the statement and database connection
```perl
$sth->finish( ) ;
$dbh->disconnect( ) ;
```

5 Save and run the program to see the tables listed

```
C:\Scripts>perl db-foreign.pl

Table 'books' added successfully!

Table 'loans' added successfully!

C:\Scripts>perl db-list.pl
Table: users
Table: sqlite_sequence
Table: books
Table: loans

C:\Scripts>_
```

Hot tip

The **sqlite_sequence** table is an internal system table that is automatically generated to keep track of the **AUTOINCREMENT** process. Once created, it cannot be deleted.

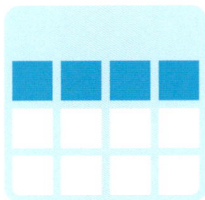

Inserting rows

A row can be inserted into a database table using the SQL query **INSERT INTO table-name (column-name, column-name) VALUES (?, ?)**. The **?** characters are placeholders for the actual values that are specified after the query statement.

The total number of table rows containing data can be obtained with the SQL query **SELECT COUNT(*) FROM table-name** in which the * asterisk character means "all".

db-insert.pl

1 Begin a Perl script by connecting to a database

```
use strict ; use warnings ; use DBI ;
my $dbh =
    DBI->connect( "dbi:SQLite:dbname=library.db",
    "", "", { RaiseError => 1 } )
    or die "Cannot connect: $DBI::errstr " ;
```

Hot tip

Once **RaiseError => 1** is set globally upon connection to the database, the **undef** keyword lets subsequent statements inherit that behavior.

2 Next, execute an SQL query to insert one table row that will produce an error message and terminate on failure

```
$dbh->do(
    "INSERT INTO users (name, email) VALUES (?, ?)",
    undef, 'Michael', 'mike@example.com' ) ;
```

3 Then, execute an SQL query to insert another table row

```
$dbh->do(
    "INSERT INTO users (name, email) VALUES (?, ?)",
    undef, 'Susan', 'sue@example.com' ) ;
```

4 Now, execute an SQL query to count the total number of rows in the table

```
my ($count) = $dbh->selectrow_array(
    'SELECT COUNT(*) FROM users' ) ;
```

5 Finally, output the row count and close the connection

```
print "\nTotal rows in users table: $count\n";
$dbh->disconnect( ) ;
```

6 Save and run the program to see the rows are inserted

```
Command Prompt    X    +  ∨              —   □   ×

C:\Scripts>perl db-insert.pl

Total rows in users table: 2
```

Multiple rows can be inserted into a database table by first defining each required value in an array. A loop can then insert rows into the table by assigning array elements to the SQL ? placeholders on each iteration.

1 Begin a Perl script by connecting to a database

```perl
use strict ; use warnings ; use DBI ;
my $dbh =
    DBI->connect( "dbi:SQLite:dbname=library.db",
    "", "", { RaiseError => 1 } )
    or die "Cannot connect: $DBI::errstr " ;
```

PL

db-many.pl

2 Next, create an array to define user values

```perl
my @users = (
    [ 'Bob', 'bob@example.com' ] ,
    [ 'Ann', 'ann@example.com' ] ,
    [ 'Caz', 'caz@example.com' ]
) ;
```

3 Now, add a loop to insert rows into the database table

```perl
foreach my $user ( @users ) {
    $dbh->do(
    "INSERT INTO users (name, email) VALUES (?, ?)" ,
    undef, $user->[0], $user->[1] ) ;
}
```

4 Then, execute an SQL query to count the total number of rows in the table using a **selectrow_array()** method to return the first row as a list of column values

```perl
my ($count) = $dbh->selectrow_array(
    "SELECT COUNT(*) FROM users" ) ;
```

5 Finally, output the row count and close the connection

```perl
print "\nTotal rows in users table: $count\n" ;
$dbh->disconnect( ) ;
```

6 Save and run the program to see multiple rows inserted

```
C:\Scripts>perl db-many.pl

Total rows in users table: 5
```

Fetching rows

The SQL query **SELECT * FROM table-name** can be used to fetch all rows from a database table. A statement handle can call its **fetchrow_hashref( )** method to get a hash reference to a single row. The hash keys are the column names, and the hash values are the corresponding table row values. Calling **fetchrow_hashref( )** in a loop can be used to output all rows until the final row is reached, upon which the method returns **undef** undefined.

db-getrows.pl

1 Begin a Perl script by connecting to a database
```
use strict ; use warnings ; use DBI ;
my $dbh =
    DBI->connect( "dbi:SQLite:dbname=library.db",
    "", "", { RaiseError => 1 } )
    or die "Cannot connect: $DBI::errstr " ;
```

2 Now, assign all rows to a statement handle
```
my $sth = $dbh->prepare( "SELECT * FROM users" ) ;
$sth->execute( ) ;
```

3 Then, output all table row values
```
while (my $row = $sth->fetchrow_hashref) {
    print "\nID: $row->{id}" ;
    print "\tName: $row->{name}" ;
    print "\tEmail: $row->{email}\n" ;
}
```

4 Finally, close the statement and database connection
```
$sth->finish( ) ;
$dbh->disconnect( ) ;
```

5 Save and run the program to see all table row data

```
Command Prompt        +  ˅                          —  □  ×

C:\Scripts>perl db-getrows.pl

ID: 1   Name: Michael   Email: mike@example.com

ID: 2   Name: Susan     Email: sue@example.com

ID: 3   Name: Bob       Email: bob@example.com

ID: 4   Name: Ann       Email: ann@example.com

ID: 5   Name: Caz       Email: caz@example.com
```

A specific single row can be retrieved from a table by appending a **WHERE =** clause to the SQL **SELECT * FROM** statement. This will select only the row containing a matching value. The database handle's **selectrow_hashref( )** method gets a hash reference to the single row. The hash keys are the column names. and the hash values are the corresponding table row values.

1 Begin a Perl script by connecting to a database
```perl
use strict ; use warnings ; use DBI ;
my $dbh =
    DBI->connect( "dbi:SQLite:dbname=library.db",
    "", "", { RaiseError => 1 } )
    or die "Cannot connect: $DBI::errstr " ;
```

db-getrow.pl

2 Select a row by ID and pass its hash reference for output
```perl
my $row = $dbh->selectrow_hashref(
    "SELECT * FROM users WHERE id = ?", undef, 1 ) ;
output ($row) ;
```

3 Next, add a subroutine to output the row values
```perl
sub output {
    print "\n$row->{id}\t$row->{name}\t$row->{email}\n";
}
```

4 Now, select a row by its "name" column value and pass its hash reference for output
```perl
$row = $dbh->selectrow_hashref(
    "SELECT * FROM users WHERE name = ?", undef, 'Ann') ;
output($row);
```

5 Finally, close the database connection
```perl
$dbh->disconnect( ) ;
```

6 Save and run the program to see single table row data

```
Command Prompt        +  ∨              —   □   ×

C:\Scripts>perl db-getrow.pl

1       Michael mike@example.com

4       Ann     ann@example.com
```

Updating rows

A row value can be updated in a database using the SQL query
UPDATE table-name SET column = value WHERE column = value.

1 Begin a Perl script by connecting to a database
```perl
use strict ; use warnings ; use DBI ;
my $dbh =
    DBI->connect( "dbi:SQLite:dbname=library.db",
    "", "", { RaiseError => 1 } )
    or die "Cannot connect: $DBI::errstr " ;
```

db-update.pl

2 Next, add a subroutine to output a current single row
```perl
sub show_user {
    my $row = $dbh->selectrow_hashref(
    "SELECT * FROM users WHERE id = ?", undef, 1) ;
    print "\n$row->{id}\t$row->{name}\t$row->{email}\n";
}
```

3 Then, output the current row and a separator line
```perl
show_user( ) ;
print '-' x 60 . "\n" ;
```

4 Now, update one value on a single row
```perl
$dbh->do(
    "UPDATE users SET name = 'Mike' WHERE id = 1") ;
```

5 Display a confirmation and output the updated row
```perl
print "Row updated successfully!" ;
show_user( ) ;
```

6 Finally, close the database connection
```perl
$dbh->disconnect( ) ;
```

7 Save and run the program to see the updated row

```
C:\Scripts>perl db-update.pl

1       Michael mike@example.com
_____
Row updated successfully!
1       Mike    mike@example.com

C:\Scripts>
```

Deleting rows

One or more rows can be deleted from a database using the SQL query **DELETE FROM table-name WHERE column IN (value, value)**.

1 Begin a Perl script by connecting to a database
```
use strict ; use warnings ; use DBI ;
my $dbh =
    DBI->connect( "dbi:SQLite:dbname=library.db",
    "", "", { RaiseError => 1 } )
    or die "Cannot connect: $DBI::errstr " ;
```

2 Next, add a subroutine to output all rows
```
sub show_all_users {
    my $sth = $dbh->prepare( "SELECT * FROM users" ) ;
    $sth->execute( ) ;
    while (my $row = $sth-> fetchrow_hashref) {
      print "$row->{id}\t$row->{name}\t$row->{email}\n";
    }
    $sth->finish( ) ;
}
```

3 Then, output all current rows and a separator line
```
show_all_users( );
print '-' x 60 . "\n" ;
```

4 Now, delete two rows, then output all remaining rows
```
$dbh->do(
    "DELETE FROM users WHERE name IN ('Ann', 'Caz')" ) ;
show_all_users( ) ;
```

5 Finally, close the database connection, then save and run the program to see the updated table
```
$dbh->disconnect( ) ;
```

db-delete.pl

Hot tip

Use the **do** method for simple **INSERT**, **UPDATE**, and **DELETE** queries, but use the **prepare** and **execute** methods for repeated execution and complex queries.

```
C:\Scripts>perl db-delete.pl
1       Mike    mike@example.com
2       Susan   sue@example.com
3       Bob     bob@example.com
4       Ann     ann@example.com
5       Caz     caz@example.com
_____

1       Mike    mike@example.com
2       Susan   sue@example.com
3       Bob     bob@example.com

C:\Scripts>
```

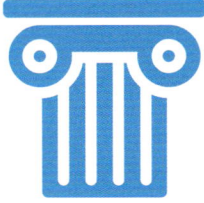

Adding columns

An existing database table can be modified using an SQL **ALTER TABLE** query to specify the name of the table. This can be followed by **ADD COLUMN** to specify the name of a column to add. Finally, the query must specify the type of data the new column can contain (**TEXT**, for example) and any field modifiers. So, the syntax might look like this:

> **ALTER TABLE table-name ADD COLUMN column-name TEXT**

If adding a **NOT NULL** constraint to the query, there must also be a **DEFAULT** value specified to fill the column for existing records. New column values can then be added by **UPDATE** queries that select each row by an existing field value.

The results of a query can be sorted based on a column specified to an **ORDER BY** clause. By default, the results are sorted alphabetically A-Z, or numerically from the smallest to the largest number.

db-addcol.pl

1 Begin a Perl script by connecting to a database

```
use strict ; use warnings ; use DBI ;
my $dbh =
    DBI->connect( "dbi:SQLite:dbname=library.db",
    "", "", { RaiseError => 1 } )
    or die "Cannot connect: $DBI::errstr " ;
```

2 Next, check that a column of the same name as the column to be added does not already exist

```
my $column_exists = $dbh->selectrow_array(
    "SELECT COUNT(*)
    FROM pragma_table_info('users')
    WHERE name = 'surname' "
    ) ;
```

3 Now, if not existing, add a new column

```
if (!$column_exists) {
    $dbh->do(
    "ALTER TABLE users
    ADD COLUMN surname
    TEXT NOT NULL DEFAULT 'Unknown' "
    ) ;
}
```

Beware

When adding a column with a **NOT NULL** constraint there must also be a **DEFAULT** value.

130

4 Then, fill the new column with data
```
$dbh->do("UPDATE users SET surname = ?
WHERE name = 'Mike'", undef, 'McGrath');

$dbh->do("UPDATE users SET surname = ?
WHERE name = 'Susan'", undef, 'Andrews');

$dbh->do("UPDATE users SET surname = ?
WHERE name = 'Bob'", undef, 'Williams');
```

5 Next, add a subroutine to output all rows
```
sub show_all_users {
    my $sth = $dbh->prepare(shift) ;
    $sth->execute( ) ;
    while ( my $row = $sth->fetchrow_hashref ) {
        print "$row->{id}\t$row->{name}" .
            "\t$row->{surname}\n" ;
    }
}
```

6 Now, output all row data, sorted in two ways
```
print "\nSorted by first name...\n" ;
show_all_users("SELECT * FROM users ORDER BY name") ;
print '-' x 60 . "\n";
print "\nSorted by last name...\n" ;
show_all_users("SELECT * FROM users ORDER BY surname") ;
```

7 Finally, close the database connection, then save and run the program to see the added table column
```
$dbh->disconnect( ) ;
```

```
C:\Scripts>perl db-addcol.pl

Sorted by first name ...
3       Bob     Williams
1       Mike    McGrath
2       Susan   Andrews
------------------------------------------------------------

Sorted by last name ...
2       Susan   Andrews
1       Mike    McGrath
3       Bob     Williams
```

Rerun the **db-explain.pl** script created previously to see the altered table structure.

131

Relating tables

Data from multiple database tables can be combined using the **PRIMARY KEY** and **FOREIGN KEY** fields. The structures of the three tables created in this chapter are shown below:

db-explains.pl

```
Command Prompt  ×   +  ∨                          —    □    ×

C:\Scripts>perl db-explains.pl

USERS ...
col        name       type       not_null  default    pk

0          id         INTEGER    0                     1
1          name       TEXT       1                     0
2          email      TEXT       1                     0
3          surname    TEXT       1         'Unknown'   0

BOOKS ...
col        name       type       not_null  default    pk

0          id         INTEGER    0                     1
1          title      TEXT       1                     0

LOANS ...
col        name       type       not_null  default    pk

0          id         INTEGER    0                     1
1          user_id    INTEGER    1                     0
2          book_id    INTEGER    1                     0

C:\Scripts>
```

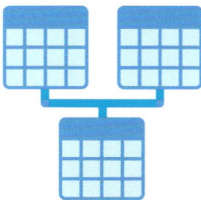

In the "loans" table, the **user_id** references the **PRIMARY KEY** of the "users" table, and the **book_id** references the **PRIMARY KEY** of the "books" table. This allows the "loans" table to keep track of who has borrowed which book. An SQL **JOIN ON** clause makes the link by specifying on which table field to assign a **PRIMARY KEY**. Its syntax looks like this:

```
JOIN foreign-table ON this-table.field = foreign-table.pk
```

The **JOIN** clauses link the tables, so can be preceded by a **SELECT** clause that can access the fields of the linked tables by stating the table name and field name, separated by a full stop, and a **FROM** clause to specify the name of the table making the link:

```
SELECT foreign-table.field, foreign-table.field, other-table.field
FROM this-table
JOIN foreign-table ON this-table.field = foreign-table.pk
JOIN other-table ON this-table.field = other-table.pk
```

...cont'd

1 Begin a Perl script by connecting to a database

```perl
use strict ; use warnings ; use DBI ;
my $dbh =
    DBI->connect( "dbi:SQLite:dbname=library.db",
    "", "", { RaiseError => 1 } )
    or die "Cannot connect: $DBI::errstr " ;
```

db-relate.pl

2 Next, add data to two empty tables

```perl
my $count = $dbh->selectrow_array(
    "SELECT COUNT(*) FROM books" );

if ($count == 0) { $dbh->do("INSERT INTO books (title)
VALUES  ('Don Quixote'), ('The Great Gatsby'), ('Moby Dick')") ;

$dbh->do("INSERT INTO loans (user_id, book_id)
VALUES (1, 2), (2, 1), (3, 3)") ; }
```

3 Now, extract data via the linking table

```perl
my $sth = $dbh->prepare(
"SELECT users.name, users.surname, books.title
FROM loans
JOIN users ON loans.user_id = users.id
JOIN books ON loans.book_id = books.id" ) ;
$sth->execute( ) ;
```

4 Now, output the extracted row data

```perl
while (my @row = $sth->fetchrow_array) {
    print "\n* $row[0] $row[1] borrowed $row[2]\n";
} ;
```

5 Finally, close the statement and database connection, then save and run the program to see the linked data

```perl
$sth->finish( ) ;
$dbh->disconnect( ) ;
```

```
Command Prompt    ×    +  ∨                          —    □    ×

C:\Scripts>perl db-relate.pl

* Mike McGrath borrowed The Great Gatsby

* Susan Andrews borrowed Don Quixote

* Bob Williams borrowed Moby Dick

C:\Scripts>_
```

Dropping tables

A table can be deleted from the database using the SQL query **DROP TABLE IF EXISTS table-name**. This action is permanent and cannot be undone, so it is a good idea to request confirmation before deleting a table.

PL

db-drop.pl

1 Begin a Perl script by connecting to a database
```perl
use strict ; use warnings ; use DBI ;
my $dbh =
    DBI->connect( "dbi:SQLite:dbname=library.db",
    "", "", { RaiseError => 1 } )
    or die "Cannot connect: $DBI::errstr " ;
```

2 Next, output a list of all tables in the database
```perl
my $sth = $dbh->prepare(
"SELECT name FROM sqlite_master WHERE type='table' ") ;
$sth->execute( ) ;
while (my ($table) = $sth->fetchrow_array) {
    print "Table: $table\n";
}
```

3 Now, create an array of table names
```perl
my @tables = ('books', 'loans', 'users') ;
```

4 Then, add a subroutine to check that a table exists
```perl
sub table_exists {
    my ($dbh, $table) = @_ ;
    my $sth = $dbh->prepare(
    "SELECT name FROM sqlite_master
    WHERE type='table' AND name=?" ) ;
    $sth->execute($table) ;
    my $exists = $sth->fetchrow_array ;
    $sth->finish( ) ;
    return $exists ;
}
```

5 Next, add a subroutine to confirm that the user wants to delete a table
```perl
sub confirm_deletion {
    my ($table) = @_ ;
    print "\nDelete '$table'? (Y/N): ";
    my $input = <STDIN>;
    chomp $input ;
    return uc($input) eq 'Y';
}
```

Hot tip

An SQLite database is simply a file, so the database can be removed by deleting the file.

...cont'd

6 Now, add a subroutine to delete a table
```perl
sub delete_table {
    my ($dbh, $table) = @_ ;
    $dbh->do("DROP TABLE IF EXISTS $table") ;
    print "Deleted '$table' successfully.\n" ;
}
```

7 Then, add a loop to delete a table if it exists and the user has confirmed deletion
```perl
foreach my $table (@tables) {
    if (table_exists($dbh, $table)) {
        if (confirm_deletion($table)) {
            delete_table($dbh, $table) ;
        }
    }
}
```

8 Finally, close the database connection
```perl
$dbh->disconnect( ) ;
```

9 Save and run the program to delete the tables

```
Command Prompt

C:\Scripts>perl db-drop.pl
Table: sqlite_sequence
Table: users
Table: books
Table: loans

Delete 'books'? (Y/N): y
Deleted 'books' successfully.

Delete 'loans'? (Y/N): n

Delete 'users'? (Y/N): y
Deleted 'users' successfully.

C:\Scripts>perl db-drop.pl
Table: sqlite_sequence
Table: loans

Delete 'loans'? (Y/N): y
Deleted 'loans' successfully.

C:\Scripts>perl db-drop.pl
Table: sqlite_sequence
```

Summary

- A database is composed of one or more tables that structure the data into organized rows and columns.

- A database table **PRIMARY KEY** is a unique identifier that identifies a record in that table.

- A database table **FOREIGN KEY** references a **PRIMARY KEY** in another table.

- The Perl **DBI** (DataBase Interface) module has a **connect** method that is used to open a database.

- The SQL query **CREATE TABLE IF NOT EXISTS** specifies a table name, column names, and column data types.

- SQLite contains an **sqlite_master** table that stores information about the database, and has a **PRAGMA table_info** function that can be used to explain a table's structure.

- The SQL query **SELECT FROM** retrieves table data, and can include a **WHERE** clause to filter the results.

- Simple SQL **INSERT**, **UPDATE**, and **DELETE** queries can be executed in Perl by the database handle's **do** method.

- Complex SQL queries can be executed in Perl by a statement handle's **prepare, execute**, and **finish** methods.

- The total number of table rows containing data can be obtained with the SQL query **SELECT COUNT(*) FROM**.

- The statement handle's **fetchrow_hashref** method returns all table rows, and its **selectrow_hashref** method gets a single row.

- An existing table can be modified by an SQL **ALTER TABLE** query, and a column added by an **ADD COLUMN** clause.

- An SQL **ORDER BY** clause can be included in a **SELECT** query to sort the results alphabetically or numerically.

- An SQL **JOIN ON** clause makes the link between tables by specifying on which table field to assign a **PRIMARY KEY**.

- The SQL query **DROP TABLE IF EXISTS** permanently deletes a table from the database.

9 Sending Web Responses

The examples in this chapter use the free Abyss Personal Edition web server available at **www.aprelium.com** Installed locally on your computer, this can be addressed by the domain name **localhost** or by the IP address **127.0.0.1**.

The Common Gateway Interface (CGI) is a standard for web servers to generate dynamic content.

Generating a web page

Whenever a user asks to view an online web page in their browser it requests the page from the web server, and receives the page in response, via the HTTP (HyperText Transfer Protocol) standard.

Where a requested web page address is an HTML document (typically with a **.html** file extension), the web server response will return that file to the browser so that its contents can be displayed.

Where Perl is installed on the computer hosting the web server, the web server can be configured to recognize Perl scripts (typically with a **.pl** file extension) and call upon the Perl interpreter to process script code before sending a response to the web server, for return to the web browser via HTTP.

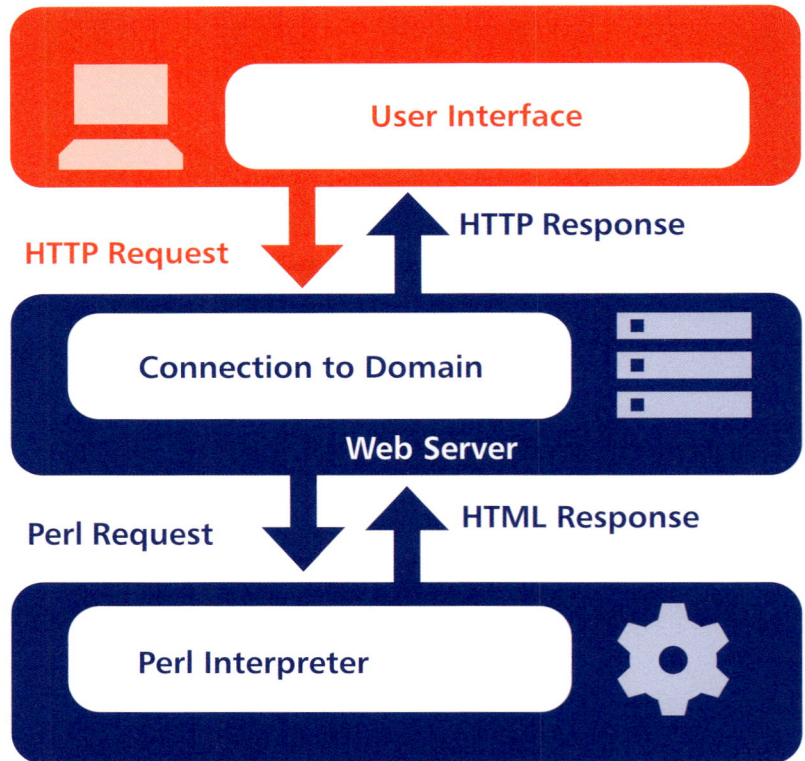

User Interface

HTTP Request   **HTTP Response**

Connection to Domain

Web Server

Perl Request   **HTML Response**

Perl Interpreter

A Perl script requested by a web browser can generate a complete HTML document response using the Perl **CGI** module to generate HTTP components and HTML elements. The web browser will parse the returned response and display content on the screen.

1 Ensure the web server is running and configured for Perl scripts, then start a script to use the **CGI** module
use strict ;
use warnings ;
use CGI ;

response.pl

Interface	Interpreter	Associated Extensions		
CGI/ISAPI	C:\Perl\perl\bin\perl.exe	pl	🖉	🗑
Windows				**Add**

Interface	Interpreter	Associated Extensions		
CGI/ISAPI	/bin/perl	pl	🖉	🗑
Linux				**Add**

2 Next, create a Perl **CGI** object and generate a HTTP header for an HTML document
my $cgi = CGI->new ;
print $cgi->header('text/html') ;

3 Now, start the HTML document by assigning a title
print $cgi->start_html(-title => 'Web Server Response') ;

4 Then, output the HTML document body containing a heading element and a paragraph element
print $cgi->h1('Hello from Perl!') ;
print $cgi->p('This HTML page is generated by Perl CGI') ;

5 Now, end the HTML document
print $cgi->end_html ;

6 Finally, save the Perl file in the web server's HTML documents directory – typically, this will be **/htdocs**

7 Open a web browser and request the script from the web server via the HTTP protocol – to see the HTML document response provided by the Perl script

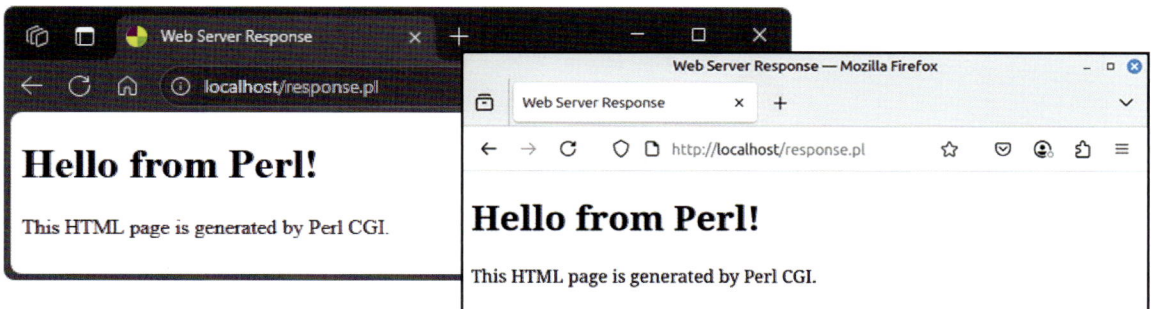

Getting values

Values can be passed to a Perl script on the web server when the browser makes an HTTP request. Those values can be used in the script and echoed in a response returned to the browser.

Perl's **CGI** module can be used to easily handle data passed from the web browser by an HTTP request. A **CGI** object receives any key-value pairs passed from the web browser. The **CGI** module provides a **param( )** method that accepts a key name as its argument and returns the associated value.

The browser can submit data to the script using a "GET" method that simply appends key-value pairs to the script's URL address. These follow a **?** question mark character after the file name, and multiple pairs must be separated by an **&** ampersand character – for example, **script.pl?key1=value1&key2=value2**.

get.html

1 Create a new HTML document containing hyperlinks with appended values to pass to a Perl script

```
<!DOCTYPE HTML>
<html lang="en">
<head>
<meta charset="UTF-8">
<title>Appended GET Values</title>
</head>
<body>
<h1>
<a href="get.pl?make=Ferrari&model=Dino">Ferrari</a>
<a href="get.pl?make=Fiat&model=Topolino">Fiat</a>
<a href="get.pl?make=Ford&model=Mustang">Ford</a>
</h1>
</body>
</html>
```

get.pl

2 Next, start a new Perl script to use the **CGI** module

```
use strict ;
use warnings ;
use CGI ;
```

3 Now, create a Perl **CGI** object and generate a HTTP header for an HTML document

```
my $cgi = CGI->new ;
print $cgi->header( 'text/html' ) ;
```

4 Then, start the HTML document by assigning a title

```
print $cgi->start_html( -title => 'Web Server Response' ) ;
```

5 Next, assign passed values to variables
```
my $make = $cgi->param( 'make' ) ;
my $model = $cgi->param( 'model' ) ;
```

6 Now, output the passed values in a response heading
```
print $cgi->h1( $make, $model ) ;
```

7 As a nicety, add a hyperlink that can be used to reload the page from which the data was sent
```
print $cgi->a( {href => $cgi->referer( ) }, 'Back' ) ;
```

8 Then, end the HTML document
```
print $cgi->end_html ;
```

9 Finally, save the Perl file in the web server's HTML documents directory – typically, **/htdocs**

10 Open a web browser and request the HTML page from the web server via the HTTP protocol – click any hyperlink to see the response from the Perl script

The **CGI referer( )** method returns the URL of the page that referred the browser to the Perl script.

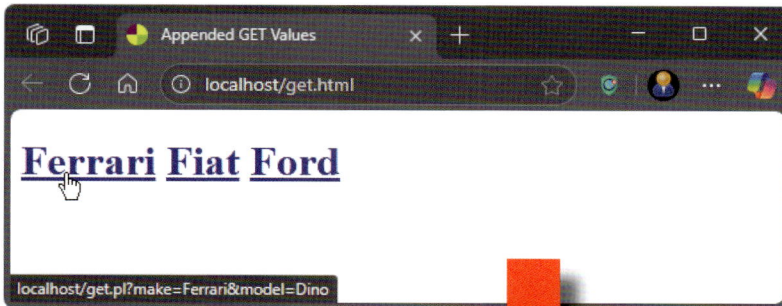

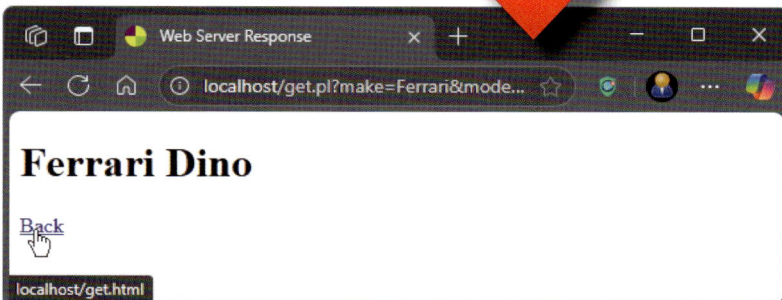

The values appended to the URL are visible in the browser address field of the response, so the GET method should not be used to send passwords or other sensitive data values to the web server.

Posting forms

Passing data from a web page to a web server using the GET method to append key-value pairs to a URL is simple, but has some limitations – the request string length cannot exceed 1024 characters, and the values appear in the browser address field.

As a more reliable alternative, the browser can submit data to the script using a "POST" method that sends the information to the web server as a separate message not appended to the URL.

Perl's **CGI** module can be used to handle form data sent from the browser with the POST method in exactly the same way as data passed from the browser with the GET method. A **CGI** object receives any key-value pairs passed from the web browser. The **CGI** module provides a **param( )** method that accepts a key name as its argument and returns the associated value.

post.html

1 Create a new HTML document containing a form with two text fields, providing default values and a submit button to post all form values to a Perl script

```html
<!DOCTYPE HTML>
<html lang="en">
<head>
<meta charset="UTF-8">
<title>Form POST Values</title>
</head>
<body>
<form method="POST" action="post.pl">
<label for="make">Make:</label>
<input type="text" name="make" value="Ford">
<label for="model">Model:</label>
<input type="text" name="model" value="Mustang">
<p><input type="submit" value="Submit"></p>
</form>
</body>
</html>
```

post.pl

2 Next, start a new Perl script to use the **CGI** module

```perl
use strict ;
use warnings ;
use CGI ;
```

3 Now, create a Perl **CGI** object and generate a HTTP header for an HTML document

```perl
my $cgi = CGI->new ;
print $cgi->header( 'text/html' ) ;
```

4 Then, start the HTML document by assigning a title
```
print $cgi->start_html( -title => 'Web Server Response' ) ;
```

5 Next, assign passed values to variables
```
my $make = $cgi->param( 'make' ) ;
my $model = $cgi->param( 'model' ) ;
```

6 Now, output the passed values in a response heading
```
print $cgi->h1( $make, $model ) ;
```

7 Add a hyperlink to reload the sending page then end the HTML document
```
print $cgi->a( {href => $cgi->referer( ) }, 'Back' ) ;
print $cgi->end_html ;
```

8 Finally, save the Perl file in the web server's HTML documents directory – typically, **/htdocs**

9 Open a web browser and request the HTML page from the web server via the HTTP protocol – click the **Submit** button to see the response from the Perl script

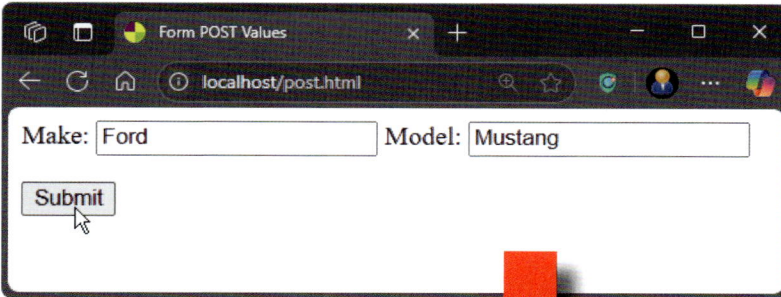

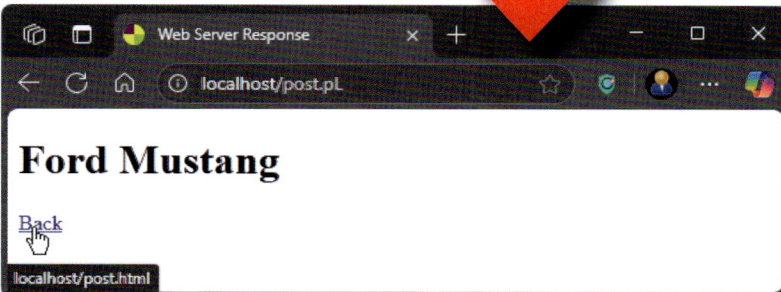

Receiving text areas

Large amounts of user-input text data can be passed from a web page to a web server using HTML **<textarea>** tags and the form POST method. **<textarea>** tags have no **value** attribute, so a default value may not be provided. It is, therefore, useful to have the Perl script test whether the text area has been left blank and provide a default value when the user has entered no text.

text.html

1 Create a new HTML document containing a form with a text area field and a submit button

```
<!DOCTYPE HTML>
<html lang="en">
<head> <meta charset="UTF-8">
<title>Text Area POST</title> </head>
<body>
<form method="POST" action="text.pl">
<textarea name="message" rows="2" cols="60">
</textarea>
<input type="submit" value="Submit">
</form>
</body>
</html>
```

text.pl

2 Next, start a new Perl script to use the **CGI** module

```
use strict ;
use warnings ;
use CGI ;
```

3 Now, create a Perl **CGI** object and generate a HTTP header for an HTML document

```
my $cgi = CGI->new ;
print $cgi->header( 'text/html' ) ;
```

4 Then, start the HTML document by assigning a title and assign a passed value to a variable

```
print $cgi->start_html( -title => 'Web Server Response' ) ;s
my $msg = $cgi->param( 'message' ) ;
```

5 Now, output the text received or a notification

```
if ( $msg eq '' ) {
    print $cgi->h3( 'No message received!' ) ;
}
else {
    print $cgi->p( $msg ) ;
}
```

...cont'd

6) Add a hyperlink to reload the sending page then end the
HTML document
```perl
print $cgi->a( {href => $cgi->referer( ) }, 'Back' ) ;
print $cgi->end_html ;
```

7) Finally, save the script then request the HTML page and
click the **Submit** button to see the Perl script's response

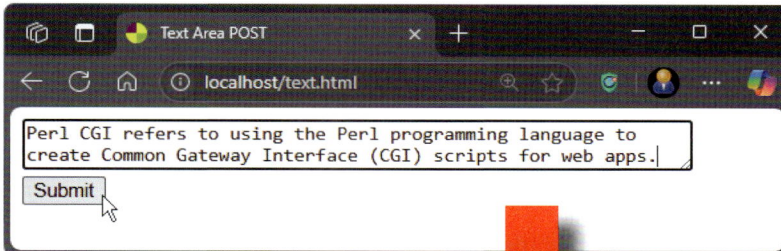

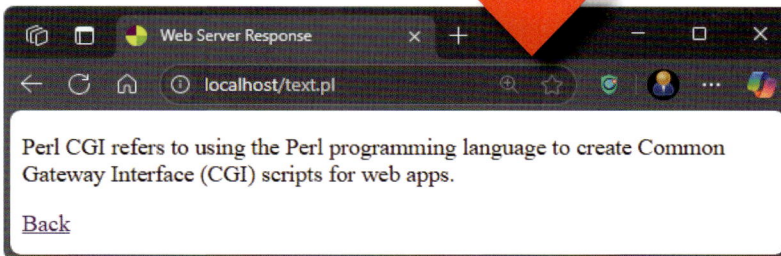

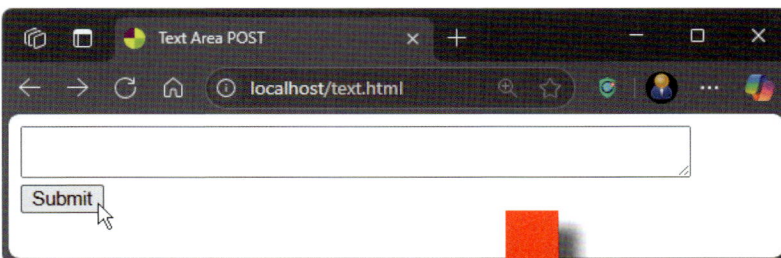

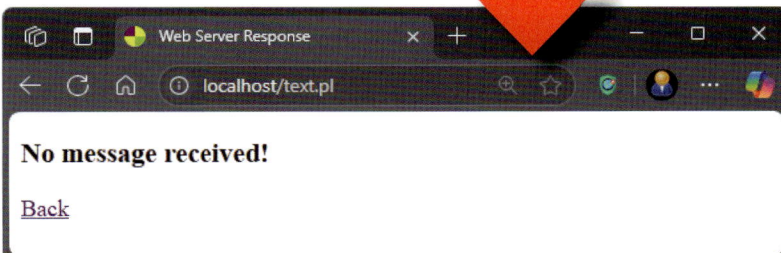

Handling check options

An HTML form can provide a visual checkbox "on/off" switch that the user can toggle to include or exclude its associated data for submission to the server. When the box is checked, the switch is set to "on" and its key-value pair will be submitted.

A checkbox is created by assigning the value "checkbox" to the **type** attribute of an **<input>** tag. This tag must also include a **name** attribute and a **value** attribute to specify the key-value pair values.

A "radio button" is similar to a checkbox but is created by assigning the value "radio" to the **type** attribute of an **<input>** tag. Unlike checkboxes, radio buttons that share a common name are mutually exclusive, so when one radio button is selected, all others in that group are automatically switched off.

Multiple checkboxes and radio buttons can be visually grouped by surrounding their **<input>** elements with **<fieldset>** **</fieldset>** tags. These may also contain **<legend>** **</legend>** tags to state a common group name.

HTML

check.html

1 Create a new HTML document containing a form with radio buttons, checkboxes, and a submit button

```
<!DOCTYPE HTML>
<html lang="en">
<head> <meta charset="UTF-8">
<title>Radio & Checkbox POST</title> </head>
<body>
<form method="POST" action="check.pl">
<p>Send Details
<input type="checkbox" name="Send" value="Details">
Supply Prices
<input type="checkbox" name="Supply" value="Prices">
</p>
<fieldset>
<legend>What kind of language is HTML?</legend>
Scripting
<input type="radio" name="HTML" value="Scripting">
Markup
<input type="radio" name="HTML" value="Markup">
<br>Programming
<input type="radio" name="HTML" value="Programming">
<input type="submit" value="Submit" style="float:right">
</fieldset>
</form>
</body>
</html>
```

2 Next, start a new Perl script to use the **CGI** module
```perl
use strict ; use warnings ; use CGI ;
```

check.pl

3 Now, create a Perl **CGI** object and generate a HTTP header for an HTML document
```perl
my $cgi = CGI->new ;
print $cgi->header( 'text/html' ) ;
print $cgi->start_html( -title => 'Web Server Response' ) ;
```

4 Then, add a loop to list all submitted key-value pairs
```perl
print "<ol>";
foreach my $key ( $cgi->param ) {
    my $value = $cgi->param( $key ) ;
    print "<li>$key $value</li>" ;
}
print "</ol>" ;
```

5 Add a hyperlink to reload the sending page then end the HTML document
```perl
print $cgi->a( {href => $cgi->referer( ) }, 'Back' ) ;
print $cgi->end_html ;
```

6 Finally, save the script then request the HTML page and click the **Submit** button to see the Perl script's response

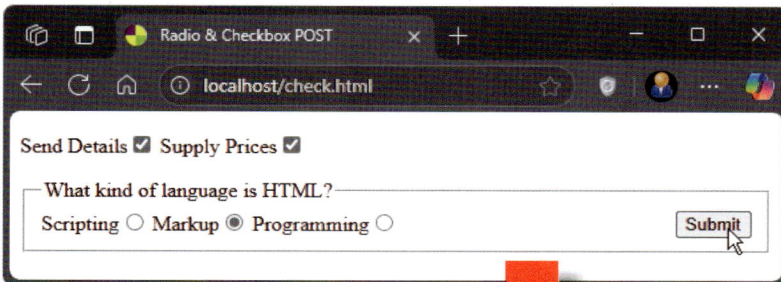

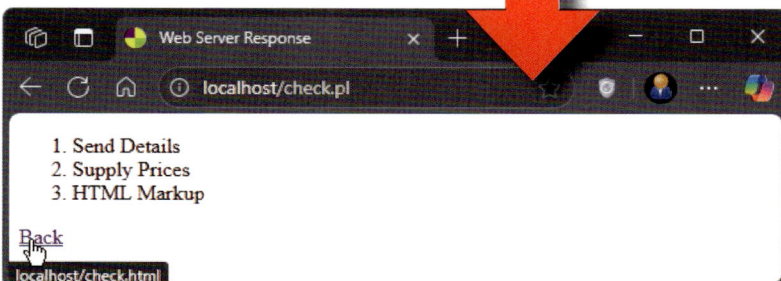

Selecting list options

An HTML form can provide a select option list, from which the user can select one option to include its associated data for submission to the server.

A select option list is created using **<select>** **</select>** tags. The opening **<select>** tag must include a **name** attribute specifying a list name. The **<select>** element encloses **<option>** **</option>** tags that define each option. Each opening **<option>** tag must include a **value** attribute specifying an option value. When the form is submitted, the list name and the selected option value are sent to the server as a key-value pair.

Optionally, one **<option>** tag may also include a Boolean **selected** attribute to automatically select that option:

select.html

1. Create a new HTML document containing a form with two drop-down option lists, and a submit button

```
<!DOCTYPE HTML>
<html lang="en">
<head> <meta charset="UTF-8">
<title>Select Option POST</title> </head>
<body>
<form method="POST" action="select.pL">
<label for="sandwich">Select a sandwich:</label>
<select name="sandwich">
<option value="Cheese">Grilled Cheese</option>
<option value="Beef">Roast Beef</option>
<option value="Chicken" selected>Grilled Chicken
</option>
</select>
<label for="drink">Choose a drink:</label>
<select name="drink">
<option value="Tea">Iced Tea</option>
<option value="Cola" selected>Pepsi Cola</option>
<option value="Juice">Orange Juice</option>
</select>
<input type="submit" value="Submit" style="float:right">
</form>
</body>
</html>
```

2 Next, start a new Perl script to use the **CGI** module
`use strict ; use warnings ; use CGI ;`

select.pl

3 Now, create a Perl **CGI** object and generate a HTTP header for an HTML document
`my $cgi = CGI->new ;`
`print $cgi->header( 'text/html' ) ;`
`print $cgi->start_html( -title => 'Web Server Response' ) ;`

4 Then, output the selected value in each option list
`print $cgi->h2( 'Your selection' ) ;`
`print $cgi->param( 'sandwich' ) . " sandwich and " ;`
`print $cgi->param( 'drink' ) . "<p>";`

5 Add a hyperlink to reload the sending page then end the HTML document
`print $cgi->a( {href => $cgi->referer( ) }, 'Back' ) ;`
`print "</p>" . $cgi->end_html ;`

6 Finally, save the script then request the HTML page and select options – hit the **Submit** button to see the Perl script's response

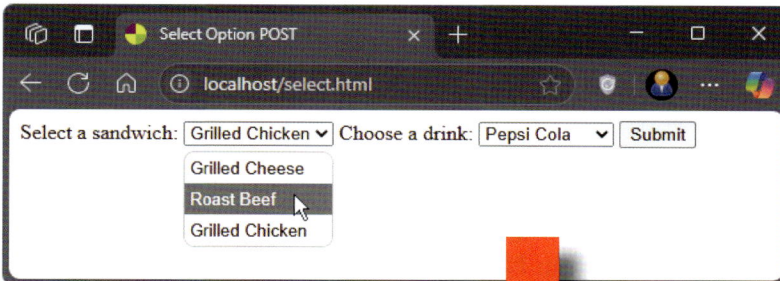

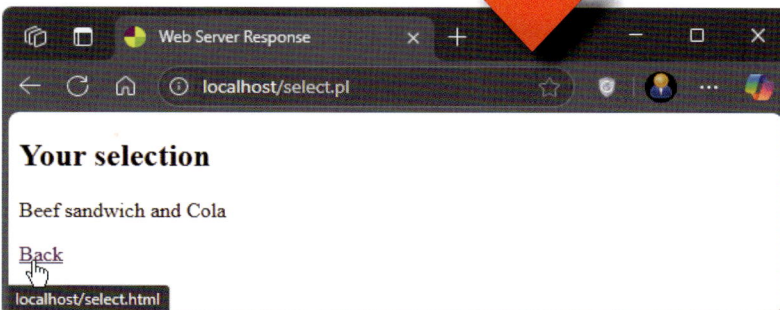

Submitting valid options

An HTML form **<input>** tag can enforce its completion by including the **required** keyword. It can also control what the user is permitted to submit by the value assigned to its **type** attribute. Restrictive input types prohibit submission of the form if the user enters a value that is not permitted and issue an error notice. Some also provide special controls that allow the user to easily select a permitted value.

permit.html

1 Create a new HTML document containing a form with four restrictive input fields, and a submit button

```
<!DOCTYPE HTML>
<html lang="en">
<head> <meta charset="UTF-8">
<title>Permitted Data POST</title> </head>
<body>
<form method="POST" action="permit.pl">
<label for="Color">Color:</label>
<input type="color" name="Color">
<label for="Range">Range:</label>
<input type="range" name="Range" min="1" max="10">
<label for="Time">Time</label>
<input type="time" name="Time"><br>
<label for="URL">URL:</label>
<input type="url" name="URL" size="30" required><p>
<input type="submit" value="Submit"></p>
</form>
</body>
</html>
```

permit.pl

2 Next, start a new Perl script to use the **CGI** module

```
use strict ; use warnings ; use CGI ;
```

3 Now, create a Perl **CGI** object and generate a HTTP header for an HTML document

```
my $cgi = CGI->new ;
print $cgi->header( 'text/html' ) ;
print $cgi->start_html( -title => 'Web Server Response' ) ;
```

4 Then, add a loop to list all submitted key-value pairs

```
print "<ol>";
foreach my $key ( $cgi->param ) {
   my $value = $cgi->param( $key ) ;
   print "<li>$key $value</li>" ;
}
print "</ol>" ;
```

5 Add a hyperlink to reload the sending page then end the HTML document

```perl
print $cgi->a( {href => $cgi->referer( ) }, 'Back' ) ;
print $cgi->end_html ;
```

6 Finally, save the script then request the HTML page

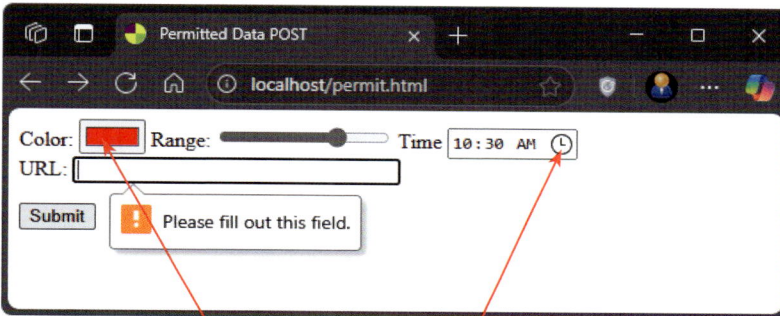

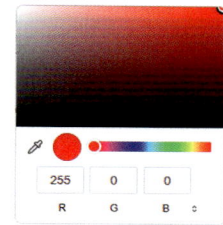

color picker

7 Click the color swatch and clock icon and use the pop-up pickers to select values, then complete other fields and hit the **Submit** button to see the Perl script's response

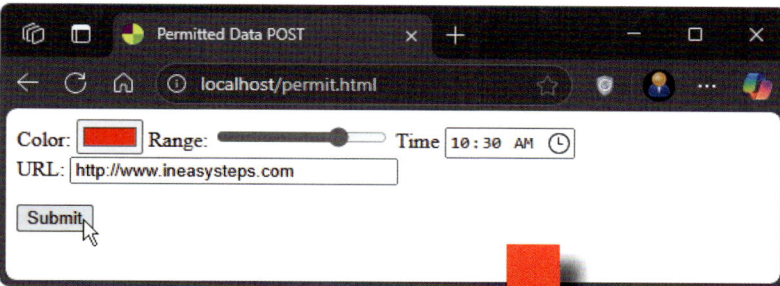

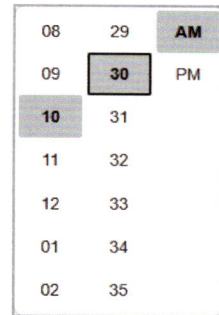

time picker

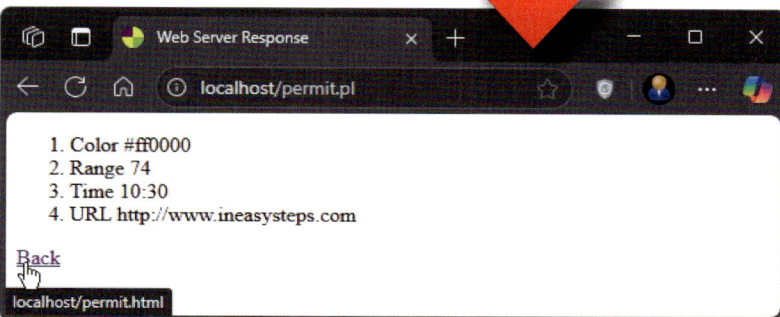

1. Color #ff0000
2. Range 74
3. Time 10:30
4. URL http://www.ineasysteps.com

Back

localhost/permit.html

Uploading files

An HTML form can provide a file selection facility by assigning the value "file" to the **type** attribute of an **<input>** tag and a name to its **name** attribute. This produces a text field and a button to launch a selection dialog. After a file has been selected, its name appears in the text field. When the form is submitted, the element name and file name are sent to the web server as a key-value pair. To upload a file the **<form>** tag must include an **enctype** attribute specifying the encoding type as "multipart/form-data". Also, its **method** attribute must specify the POST method – because form data cannot be appended to a URL using the GET method.

A Perl script can use a CGI **upload** method to obtain a file handle to an uploaded file and a **basename** method from a **File::Basename** module to extract the filename, without any path. The **open** method can then open a new file for writing into at a chosen location and binary files, such as images or PDFs, can be written using a **binmode** method:

upload.html

1 Create an HTML document with a form element containing a file upload button and a submit button

```
<!DOCTYPE HTML>
<html lang="en">
<head> <meta charset="UTF-8">
<title>File Upload POST</title> </head>
<body>
<form method="POST" action="upload.pl"
                        enctype="multipart/form-data">
<h2>Select a file to upload:</h2>
<input type="file" name="upload_file">
<p><input type="submit" value="Upload"></p>
</form>
</body>
</html>
```

upload.pl

2 Next, start a new Perl script to use the **CGI** and **File::Basename** modules

```
use strict ; use warnings ; use CGI ; use File::Basename ;
```

3 Now, create a Perl **CGI** object and generate a HTTP header for an HTML document

```
my $cgi = CGI->new ;
print $cgi->header( 'text/html' ) ;
print $cgi->start_html( -title => 'Web Server Response' ) ;
```

4 Initialize variables with destination, file name and handle
```perl
my $upload_dir = 'C:/Abyss Web Server/htdocs/images' ;
my $filename = $cgi->param( 'upload_file' ) ;
my $fh = $cgi->upload( 'upload_file' ) ;
```

5 Then, attempt to upload the file to the destination
```perl
if ( $fh && $filename ) {
    my $basename = basename( $filename ) ;
    my $filepath = "$upload_dir/$basename" ;
    if ( open( my $out, '>', $filepath ) ) {
        binmode $out ;
        while ( my $line = <$fh> ) { print $out $line ; }
        close $out ;
        print "<h2>Uploaded: $basename</h2>" ;
    } else { print "<p>Failed to save file: $!</p>" ; }
else { print "<p>No file uploaded.</p>" ; }
```

6 Add a hyperlink then end the HTML document
```perl
print $cgi->a( {href => $cgi->referer( ) }, 'Back' ) ;
print $cgi->end_html ;
```

7 Finally, save the script then request the HTML page and choose a file to upload to the web server

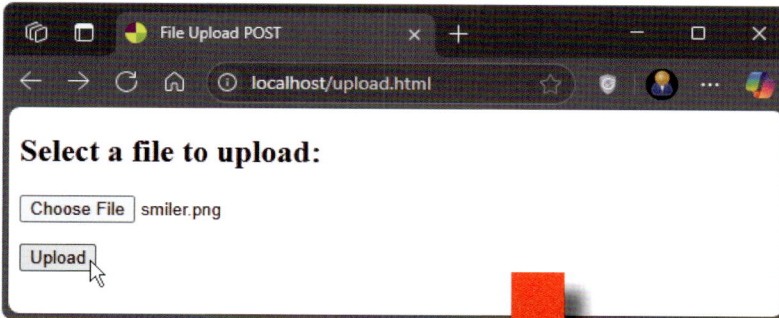

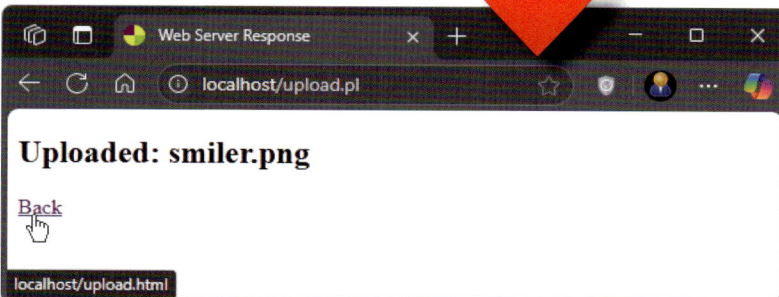

Baking cookies

Websites can store small amounts of data on your device in "cookie" files. These are text files typically limited to a maximum size of just 4096 bytes (4KB) with the following attributes:

- **name** – the key for the cookie.

- **value** – the data stored.

- **expires** – when the cookie should be deleted.

- **path** – the URL path for which the cookie is valid.

The Perl **CGI** module allows the **expires** value to be stated as a relative time string, For example **'+1d'** for one day, **'+1h'** for one hour, **'+30m'** for 30 minutes. Stating a past time will delete the cookie immediately. If the **expires** attribute is omitted, the cookie will expire when the session ends.

The **path** attribute can be used to restrict the browser to only send the cookie to the server only for requests to a specified path. To allow the cookie to be sent for site-wide requests, this can be **'/'**.

When a cookie is sent to the server in a request, its **value** data can be read in subsequent requests. To allow a cookie to be sent and immediately read, the **CGI redirect** method can reload the page.

PL

cookie.pl

1 Start a new Perl script to use the **CGI** module
```perl
use strict ; use warnings ; use CGI ;
```

2 Next, create a Perl **CGI** object and initialize variables to store the form and cookie data
```perl
my $cgi = CGI->new ;
my $send = $cgi->param( 'send' ) ;
my $user = $cgi->param( 'user' ) ;
my $auth = $cgi->cookie( 'auth' ) ;
my $cookie ;
```

3 Now, add a conditional test to set a cookie and reload the page so that the cookie data can be read immediately
```perl
if ( $send eq 'Login' && $user ) {
    $cookie = $cgi->cookie( -name => 'auth',
        -value => $user, -expires => '+1d', path => '/' ) ;
    print $cgi->redirect( -uri => $cgi->url,
        -cookie => $cookie ) ;
    exit ;
}
```

...cont'd

4 Then, add a conditional test to delete the cookie and reload the page

```perl
if ( $send eq 'Logout' ) {
    $cookie = $cgi->cookie( -name => 'auth',
        -value => $user, -expires => '-1d', path => '/' ) ;
    print $cgi->redirect( -uri => $cgi->url,
        -cookie => $cookie ) ; exit ; }
```

5 Create an HTTP header for an HTML document

```perl
print $cgi->header( 'text/html' ) ;
print $cgi->start_html( -title => 'Web Server Response' ) ;
```

6 Next, create forms to allow users to log in and out, then end the HTML document

```perl
if ( !$auth ) {
    print $cgi->start_form( -method => 'POST' ) ,
    $cgi->textfield( -name => 'user' ) ,
    $cgi->submit( -name => 'send', -value => 'Login' ) ,
    $cgi->end_form ;
} else {
    print "<h2>$auth is logged in</h2>" ,
    $cgi->start_form( -method => 'POST' ) ,
    $cgi->submit( -name => 'send', -value => 'Logout' ) ,
    $cgi->end_form ;
}
print $cgi->end_html ;
```

7 Finally, save the script then request the HTML page and use the forms to save and delete a cookie

Understanding CSRF

Cross-Site Request Forgery (CSRF) is a technique that allows malicious attackers to impersonate a legitimate user. The attacker will trick the user into logging in to a website with their valid credentials but will also perform a fraudulent transaction.

Forged GET request

A user might wish to transfer $1,000 from their bank account to a family member via a web application that has a CSRF vulnerability. An attacker has identified this vulnerability and will attempt to divert the transfer to their own account. The original request might look like this:

```
GET http://acmebank.com/transfer?acct=1234&sum=1000
```

and the attacker's forged request could look like this:

```
GET http://acmebank.com/transfer?acct=2334&sum=1000
```

Now, the attacker will try to trick the user into sending the forged request, perhaps by sending an email to the user pretending to be from the user's bank:

```
From: AcmeBank
Dear client,
We have a free gift for you. Just click here to receive it.
```

Here, the link executes the forged request and diverts the transfer.

Forged POST request

If the bank's web application uses POST requests, the attacker could create a form with the forged request, like this:

```
<form method="POST" action="http://acmebank/transfer">
<input type="hidden" name="acct" value="2334">
<input type="hidden" name="sum" value="1000">
<input type="submit" value="Click to get your free gift">
</form>
```

Here, the submit button executes the forged request and diverts the transfer. Even more sneaky, the form could automatically submit the forged request by removing the submit button element and adding a snippet of JavaScript code:

```
<script> document.forms[0].submit(); </script>
```

Now, the forged request is executed when the user visits the page.

Keeping a secret

Prevention of CSRF attacks is enabled by passing a unique unpredictable token to the server for validation. A CSRF token is embedded in a form or requests to ensure the request is legitimate. The Perl **WWW::CSRF** module provides a method named **generate_csrf_token** that can be used to create a token. This requires two arguments to specify the user identity and a "secret". The secret is a key that is used by the method to generate a tamper-proof cryptographic string describing the user, and a timestamp.

A static secret can be stored in a file, but for security this must not be located in the server's root directory **/htdocs**. It could, instead, be located in a **/csrf** directory adjacent to the **/htdocs** directory. The file can simply return a hash reference when called.

```
# csrf/secret.pl
return {
    csrf_secret => 'SecretKey123' ;
}
```

The secret can then be returned to a variable in a file within the **/htdocs** directory using **do ../csrf/secret.pl**. A secret can also be stored in an environment variable. For example, on Windows:

1 Hit the **Windows** key (**WinKey**) and enter "env" – to launch the "System Properties" dialog

2 On the Advanced tab, hit the **Environment Variables** button – to launch the "Environment Variables" dialog

3 In the User Variables category, hit the **New** button – to launch the "New User Variable" dialog

4 Enter a **CSRF_SECRET** name and a value, then hit the **OK** button – to create a secret that can be assigned to a variable in a file using **$ENV{ 'CSRF_SECRET' }**

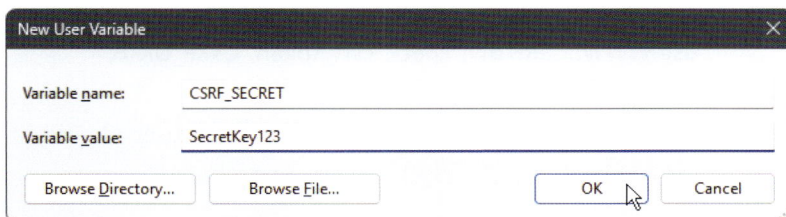

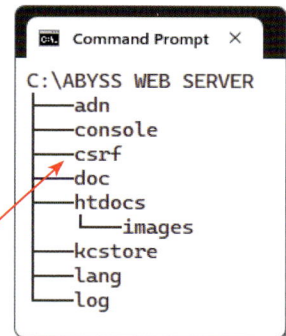

secret.pl

Hot tip

Linux users can create an environment variable to store a secret by adding a line to the shell configuration file (.bashrc, .zshrc, etc.). For example using **export CSRF_SECRET = "SecretKey123"**

Validating tokens

Having created a CSRF secret on page 157, the **WWW::CSRF** module's **generate_csrf_token** and **check_csrf_token** methods can be used to pass a token to the web server for validation against a **CSRF_OK** constant. The token is incorporated in a hidden form element for server processing upon receipt.

csrf-gen.pl

1 Start a new Perl script to use the **CGI** module and a method from the **WWW::CSRF** module
```
use strict ; use warnings ; use CGI ;
use WWW::CSRF qw( generate_csrf_token ) ;
```

2 Next, create a Perl **CGI** object and initialize a variable with a user identity
```
my $cgi = CGI->new ;
my $user = 'Mike' ;
```

3 Now, initialize a variable with a secret key
```
my $secret = ( do ../csrf/secret.pl ) -> { csrf_secret } ;
# OR: my $secret = $ENV{CSRF_SECRET} ;
```

4 Then, generate a CSRF token
```
my $token = generate_csrf_token( $user, $secret ) ;
```

5 Finally, create a form that will submit the CSRF token
```
print $cgi->header( 'text/html' ) ,
    $cgi->start_html( -title => 'CSRF Token' ) ,
    $cgi->h2( "Sending Form for $user" ) ,
    $cgi->start_form( -method => 'POST',
                      -action => 'csrf-chk.pl' ) ,
    $cgi->hidden( -name => 'token', -value => $token ) ,
    $cgi->submit ,
    $cgi->end_form ,
    $cgi->end_html ;
}
```

csrf-chk.pl

6 Save the file then start a new script to use the **CGI** module and a method and constant from the **WWW::CSRF** module
```
use strict ; use warnings ; use CGI ;
use WWW::CSRF qw( check_csrf_token, CSRF_OK ) ;
```

7 Create a **CGI** object and a variable with the user identity
```
my $cgi = CGI->new ;
my $user = 'Mike' ;
```

...cont'd

8 Now, initialize a variable with a secret key
```
my $secret = ( do ../csrf/secret.pl ) -> { csrf_secret } ;
# OR: my $secret = $ENV{CSRF_SECRET} ;
```

9 Next, obtain the submitted token and check its status
```
my $token = $cgi->param( 'token' ) ;
my $status = check_csrf_token( $user, $secret, $token ) ;
```

10 Finally, output an appropriate response
```
if ( $status == CSRF_OK ) {
    print $cgi->header( 'text/html' ) ,
    $cgi->start_html( -title => 'Web Server Response' ) ,
    $cgi->h2( "Form Received for $user" ) ,
    $cgi->end_html ;
} else {
    print $cgi->header( -status => '403 Forbidden',
                        -type => 'text/html' ) ,
    $cgi->start_html( -title => 'Forbidden' ) ,
    $cgi->h2( 'Error 403: CSRF token is invalid or expired.') ,
    $cgi->end_html ;
}
```

11 Save the file then open the page by form submission and
by direct entry to see validation succeed and fail

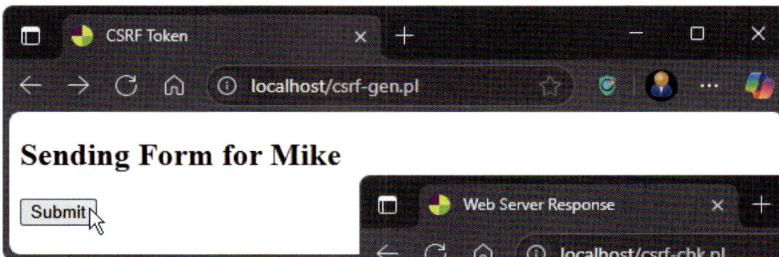

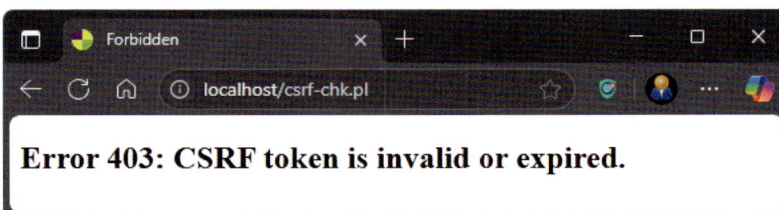

Summary

- Web browsers send requests to a web server and receive a response from the web server via HTTP.

- A web server can be configured to call upon the Perl interpreter to process script code before sending a response.

- The Perl **CGI** module can generate HTTP components and HTML elements in response to web browser requests.

- The **CGI** module's **param( )** method accepts a key name as its argument and returns the associated value.

- Data submitted to a web server via the **GET** method is appended to the URL as key-value pairs.

- Data submitted to a web server via the **POST** method is sent as a separate message, not appended to the URL.

- Most HTML form elements assign key-value pairs to **name** and **value** attributes.

- The HTML **<textarea>** element has only a **name** attribute, and the text content is the associated value.

- Some HTML form elements can control permitted content for submission.

- The Perl **File::Basename** module's **basename** method can extract the file name from a path when uploading files.

- Websites can store small amounts of data on your device in cookie files that have **name, value, expires,** and **path** attributes.

- Cookies that omit an **expires** value will expire when the session ends, and specifying a past time will delete the cookie.

- Cross-Site Request Forgery (CSRF) is a technique that allows malicious attackers to impersonate a legitimate user.

- A CSRF token is embedded in a form or requests to ensure a request to the web server is made from the legitimate user.

- The Perl **WWW::CSRF** module's **generate_csrf_token** method creates a CSRF token using a secret key.

- The Perl **WWW::CSRF** module's **_csrf_tokchecken** method validates a CSRF token against a **CSRF_OK** constant.

10 Creating Online Shops

Providing support

A basic online shopping website will typically use a database with at least these three essential tables:

- **Users** – providing a unique ID for each user, a name or email address, and a password.

- **Items** – providing a unique ID for each product offered, product name and details, and the product's price.

- **Orders** – providing a unique ID for each order, the ID of the user placing the order, the ID of the product being ordered, the quantity of items being ordered, and the payment status.

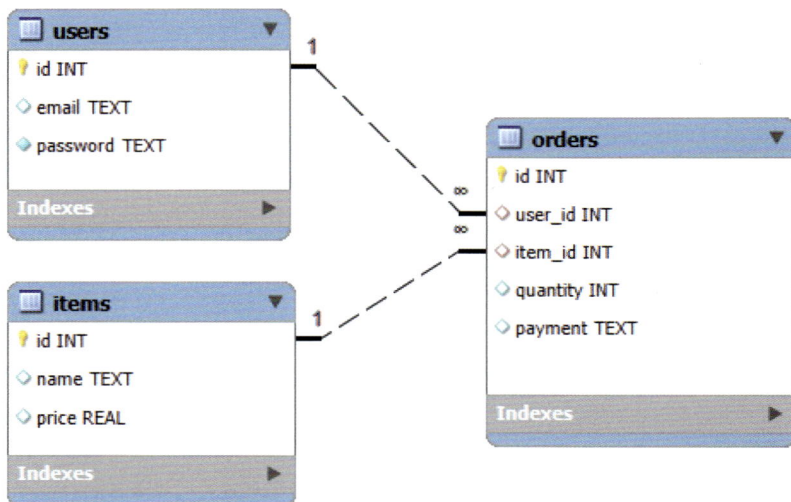

Each page of the basic online shopping website can be provided with access to common Perl modules specified in a "header" file:

- **DBI** – providing database interaction.

- **CGI** – providing web input/output ability.

- **Digest::SHA** – providing encryption for passwords using SHA (Secure Hash Algorithm) digests.

The header file is then included at the start of each page of the website by stating its location after the Perl **require** keyword.

Additionally, the header file can supply a new **CGI** object to each page, and automatically provide access to the database.

The examples in this chapter demonstrate a basic online shopping site that would benefit from security enhancements for actual production usage.

1 Begin a Perl script by enforcing strict variable declarations
```perl
use strict ;
```

2 Enable warnings to catch issues during development
```perl
use warnings ;
```

3 Load the DBI module for database interaction
```perl
use DBI ;
```

4 Load the CGI module for web input/output
```perl
use CGI ;
```

5 Load the **Digest::SHA** module and import its function for password encryption into a hexadecimal string
```perl
use Digest::SHA qw( sha256_hex ) ;
```

6 Create a CGI object to manage passed parameters and to output HTML content
```perl
our $cgi = CGI->new ;
```

7 Attempt to connect to an SQLite database that will be located in a file named "shop-db.pl"
```perl
our $dbh = DBI->connect(
    "dbi:SQLite:dbname=shop.db",
    "", "", { RaiseError => 1 } )
    or die "Cannot connect: $DBI::errstr" ;
```

8 Save the file named as "shop-hdr.pl" in the web server's HTML documents directory – typically, **/htdocs**

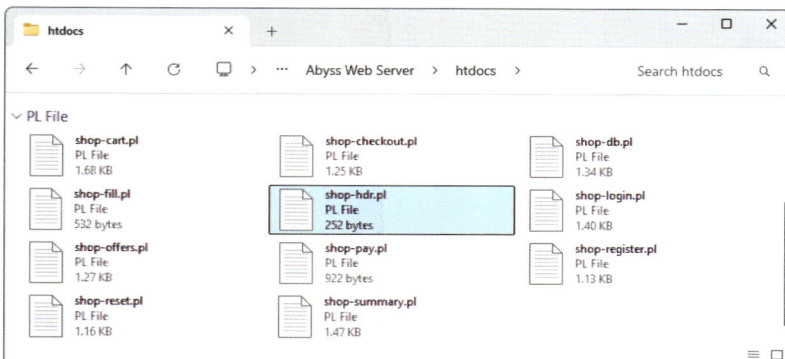

shop-hdr.pl

The Perl files shown in this screenshot comprise the entire online website example – each file will be described and listed in this chapter.

163

Creating the database

Having established support for the Perl DBI and CGI modules in the header file on page 163, the database schema can now be created by adding tables.

PL

shop-db.pl

1 Begin a Perl script by acquiring support, supplying an HTTP text header, and connecting to the database

```perl
require './shop-hdr.pl' ;
print $cgi->header( 'text/plain' ) ;
print "Connected to SHOP DATABASE successfully!" ;
```

2 Next, add a table to store user records

```perl
$dbh->do( "CREATE TABLE IF NOT EXISTS users (
    id INTEGER PRIMARY KEY AUTOINCREMENT,
    email TEXT UNIQUE NOT NULL,
    password TEXT NOT NULL)" ) ;
print "\nTable:\t'users' created successfully!" ;
```

3 Now, add a table to store product item records

```perl
$dbh->do( "CREATE TABLE IF NOT EXISTS items (
    id INTEGER PRIMARY KEY AUTOINCREMENT
    name TEXT UNIQUE NOT NULL,
    price REAL NOT NULL)" ) ;
print "\nTable:\t'items' created successfully!" ;
```

4 Then, add a table to store order records

```perl
$dbh->do("CREATE TABLE IF NOT EXISTS orders
    id INTEGER PRIMARY KEY AUTOINCREMENT,
    user_id INTEGER NOT NULL,
    item_id INTEGER NOT NULL,
    quantity INTEGER NOT NULL,
    payment TEXT DEFAULT 'Unpaid',
    FOREIGN KEY(user_id) REFERENCES users(id),
    FOREIGN KEY(item_id) REFERENCES items(id) ) " ) ;
print "\nTable:\t'orders' created successfully!\n" ;
```

5 Create a subroutine to output table schemas

```perl
sub explain {
    my ( $sth, $title ) = @_ ;
    printf "\n$title...\n" . "%-10s" x 6 . "\n" ,
        qw( col name type not_null default pk ) ;
    print "-" x 60, "\n" ;
    while ( my @row = $sth->fetchrow_array ) {
        $_ //= " for @row ;
        printf "%-10s" x 6 . "\n", @row ;
    }
}
```

...cont'd

6 Finally, add a loop to output each table's columns, then close the database connection

```perl
for my $tbl ( qw(users items orders)) {
    my $sth = $dbh->prepare("PRAGMA table_info($tbl)") ;
    $sth->execute( ) ;
    explain( $sth, uc $tbl ) ;
    $sth->finish ;
}
$dbh->disconnect ;
```

7 Save the file named as "shop-db.pl" in the web server's **/htdocs** directory, then open it via HTTP in a web browser to see the database tables

```
localhost/shop-db.pl

Connected to SHOP DATABASE successfully!
Table:  'users' created successfully!
Table:  'items' created successfully!
Table:  'orders' created successfully!

USERS...
col       name       type      not_null  default  pk
---------------------------------------------------------
0         id         INTEGER   0                  1
1         email      TEXT      1                  0
2         password   TEXT      1                  0

ITEMS...
col       name       type      not_null  default  pk
---------------------------------------------------------
0         id         INTEGER   0                  1
1         name       TEXT      1                  0
2         price      REAL      1                  0

ORDERS...
col       name       type      not_null  default  pk
---------------------------------------------------------
0         id         INTEGER   0                  1
1         user_id    INTEGER   1                  0
2         item_id    INTEGER   1                  0
3         quantity   INTEGER   1                  0
4         payment    TEXT      0         'Unpaid'  0
```

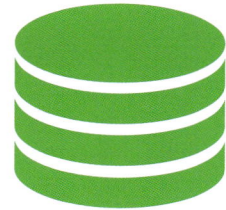

Filling product items

Having created the database tables on page 165, data can now be inserted into a table to specify available products items.

PL

shop-fill.pl

1 Begin a Perl script by acquiring support, supplying an HTTP text header, and inserting table data

```
require './shop-hdr.pl' ;
print $cgi->header('text/plain') ;
$dbh->do( "INSERT INTO items (name, price) VALUES
    ( 'Laptop', 1000 ), ( 'Smartphone', 500 ),
    ( 'Headphones', 100 ) ON CONFLICT DO NOTHING" ) ;
```

2 Next, for explanation, retrieve the inserted data and the table column headings

```
my $sth = $dbh->prepare( "SELECT * FROM items" ) ;
$sth->execute( ) ;
my @columns = @{ $sth->{NAME_lc} } ;
```

Hot tip

The DBI module provides the special **NAME_lc** attribute that is an array reference containing the table column names.

3 Then, output the table headings and contents

```
print "ITEMS VALUES...\n" ;
printf "%-5s %-20s %-10s\n", @columns ;
print "-" x 40, "\n";
while ( my $row = $sth->fetchrow_arrayref ) {
    printf "%-5s %-20s %-10s\n", @$row ;
}
```

166

Don't forget

ON CONFLICT DO NOTHING is an SQL clause to handle situations where INSERT might violate a unique constraint or primary key.

4 Finally, close the statement handle and database connection

```
$sth->finish ;
$dbh->disconnect ;
```

5 Save the file named as "shop-fill.pl" in the web server's **/htdocs** directory, then open it via HTTP in a web browser to see the table data

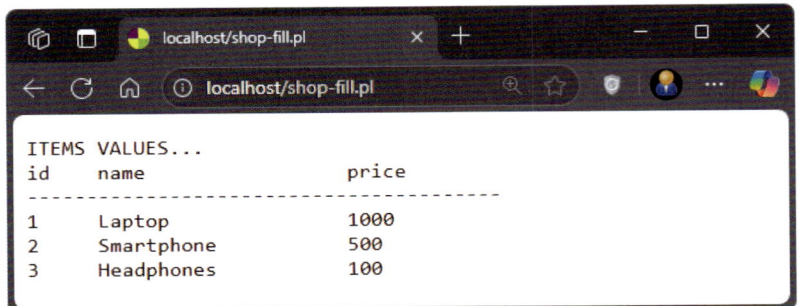

```
localhost/shop-fill.pl

ITEMS VALUES...
id      name                  price
----------------------------------------
1       Laptop                1000
2       Smartphone            500
3       Headphones            100
```

Allowing login

Now that the database setup is complete, a login page can be created to allow users to access the online shop. This will require the ability to handle a variety of validity conditions.

1 Begin a Perl script by acquiring support, and supplying an HTTP HTML header, page title and CSS style

```perl
require './shop-hdr.pl' ;
print $cgi->header( 'text/html' ) ;
print $cgi->start_html( -title => 'Online Shop' ) ;
print $cgi->style( 'a{margin-right:15px}' ) ;
```

shop-login.pl

2 Next, attempt to assign CGI parameter values to variables

```perl
my $email    = $cgi->param( 'email' ) ;
my $password = $cgi->param( 'password' ) ;
```

3 Now, add a conditional test to call appropriate subroutines if the variables have or have not received parameter values

```perl
if ( $email && $password ) {
    handle_login( $email, $password ) ;
}
else {
    show_login_form( ) ;
}
```

4 Then, close the HTML page and database connection

```perl
print $cgi->end_html ;
$dbh->disconnect ;
```

5 Add a subroutine to display a login form and options to register or reset a password

```perl
sub show_login_form {
    print $cgi->style( 'span{width:80px;display:inline-block}' ) ;
    print $cgi->start_form ;
    print $cgi->h2( 'Login' ) ;
    print $cgi->p( $cgi->span( 'Email:' ) ,
        $cgi->textfield( 'email' ) ) ;
    print $cgi->p( $cgi->span( 'Password:' ) ,
        $cgi->password_field( 'password' ) ) ;
    print $cgi->submit( 'Login' ) , "<hr>" ;
    $cgi->end_form ;

    print $cgi->p(
        $cgi->a( {-href => 'shop-register.pl' } , 'Register' ) ,
        $cgi->a( {-href => 'shop-reset.pl' } ,
                                'Reset Password' ) ) ;
}
```

...continues on the next page

...cont'd

6 Next, add a subroutine to attempt to log in a user and confirm success or failure

```perl
sub handle_login {
    my ( $email, $password ) = @_ ;
    $password = sha256_hex( $password ) ;

    my $sth = $dbh->prepare(
    "SELECT id FROM users WHERE email = ?
    AND password = ?" ) ;
    $sth->execute( $email, $password ) ;

    if ( my $id = $sth->fetchrow_array ) {
        show_success( $id ) ;
    }
    else {
        show_login_error( ) ;
    }
}
```

7 Now, add a subroutine to report login failure

```perl
sub show_login_error {
    print $cgi->h2( 'Invalid email or password.' ) ;
    print $cgi->a( { -href => 'shop-login.pl' } ,
        'Retry Login' ) , " " ;
    print $cgi->a( { -href => 'shop-register.pl' } ,
        'Register' ) ;
}
```

8 Finally, add a subroutine to report login success, and to forward the user ID when proceeding to the shop page

```perl
sub show_success {
    my ( $user_id ) = @_ ;
    print $cgi->h2( 'Login successful!' ) ;
    print $cgi->start_form( -method => 'POST',
                            -action => 'shop-offers.pl' ) ,
        $cgi->hidden( -name => 'user_id' ,
                            -value => $user_id ) ,
        $cgi->submit( 'Enter Shop' ) ,
        $cgi->end_form ;
}
```

9 Save the file named as "shop-login.pl" in the web server's **/htdocs** directory

Logging-in a user

With the database loaded and a login form available, a user can now attempt to log in to the online shop.

1 Open the "shop-login.pl" page via HTTP in a web browser to see the login form

2 Enter your email address and a password into the login form, then hit the **Login** button to see the attempt fail

3 Registered users who may have simply input their details incorrectly can hit the **Retry Login** button to return to the login form otherwise, as a new user, hit the **Register** button to open a registration page

Enabling registration

Before a user can enter the online shop, they must register with their email address and a chosen password.

shop-register.pl

1 Begin a Perl script by acquiring support, and supplying an HTTP HTML header and an HTML page title

```perl
require './shop-hdr.pl' ;
print $cgi->header( 'text/html' ) ;
print $cgi->start_html( -title => 'Online Shop' ) ;
```

2 Next, attempt to assign CGI parameter values to variables

```perl
my $email    = $cgi->param( 'email' ) ;
my $password = $cgi->param( 'password' ) ;
```

3 Now, add a conditional test to call appropriate subroutines if the variables have or have not received parameter values

```perl
if ( $email && $password ) {
    handle_registration( $email, $password ) ;
}
else {
    show_registration_form( ) ;
}
```

4 Then, close the HTML page and database connection

```perl
print $cgi->end_html ;
$dbh->disconnect ;
```

5 Add a subroutine to display a registration form

```perl
sub show_registration_form {
    print $cgi->style( 'span{width:80px;display:inline-block }' ) ;
    print $cgi->start_form ;
        print $cgi->h2( 'Registration' ) ;
        print $cgi->p( $cgi->span( 'Email:' ) ,
            $cgi->textfield( 'email' ) ) ;
        print $cgi->p( $cgi->span( 'Password:' ) ,
            $cgi->password_field( 'password' ) ) ;
        print $cgi->submit( 'Register' ) ;
    print $cgi->end_form ;
}
```

6 Add a subroutine to advise the user if they are already registered

```perl
sub show_already_registered {
    print $cgi->h2( 'User is already registered!' ) ;
    print $cgi->a( { -href => 'shop-login.pl' } , 'Login' ) ;
}
```

7 Now, add a subroutine to attempt to register the user

```perl
sub handle_registration {
    my ( $email, $password ) = @_ ;
    my $sth_check = $dbh->prepare(
    "SELECT COUNT(*) FROM users WHERE email = ?" ) ;
    $sth_check->execute( $email ) ;
    my ( $count ) = $sth_check->fetchrow_array ;

    if ( $count > 0 ) {
        show_already_registered( ) ;
    }
    else {
        my $sth = $dbh->prepare(
        "INSERT INTO users (email, password) VALUES (?, ?)" ) ;
        $password = sha256_hex( $password ) ;
        $sth->execute( $email, $password ) ;
        show_registration_success( ) ;
    }
}
```

8 Finally, add a subroutine to confirm successful registration

```perl
sub show_registration_success {
    print $cgi->h2( 'Registration successful!' ) ;
    print $cgi->a( { -href => 'shop-login.pl' } , 'Login' ) ;
}
```

9 Save the file named as "shop-register.pl" in the web server's **/htdocs** directory, then hit the **Register** button on the **Login** page to see the registration form

Browser window showing localhost/shop-register.pl

Registration

Email: [   ]

Password: [   ]

[Register]

Registering a user

With the database loaded and a registration form available, a user can now attempt to register to the online shop.

1 Enter your email address and a password into the registration form, then hit the **Register** button to see the attempt succeed

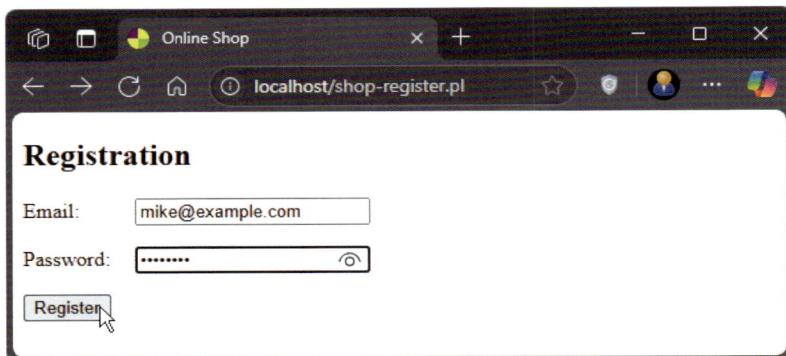

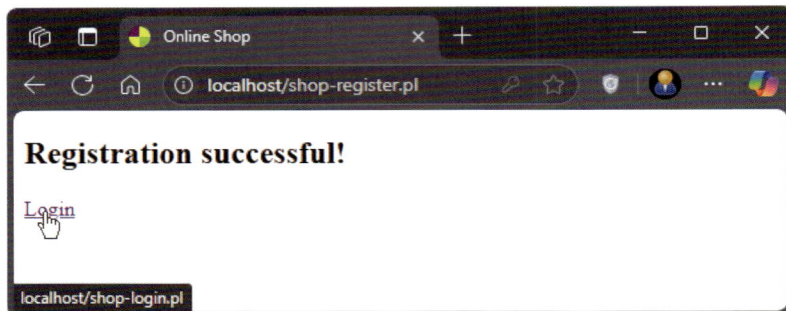

2 Return to the registration page and enter your details, then hit the **Register** button to see the attempt fail

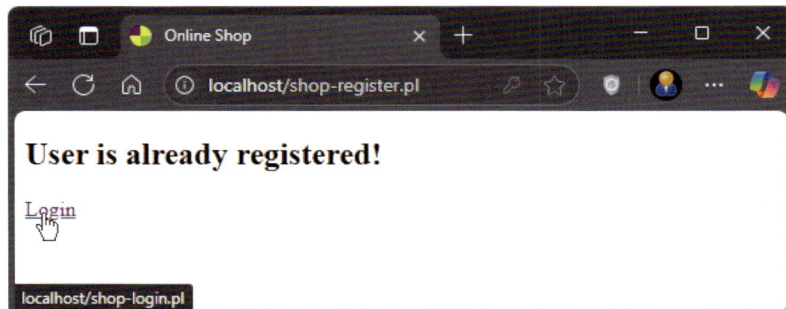

Resetting passwords

After successful registration, a user on the login page may choose to reset their password using the "Reset Password" link.

1 Begin a Perl script by acquiring support, and supplying an HTTP HTML header and an HTML page title

```perl
require './shop-hdr.pl' ;
print $cgi->header( 'text/html' ) ;
print $cgi->start_html( -title => 'Online Shop' ) ;
```

shop-reset.pl

2 Next, attempt to assign CGI parameter values to variables

```perl
my $email    = $cgi->param( 'email' ) ;
my $password = $cgi->param( 'new_password' ) ;
```

3 Now, add a conditional test to call appropriate subroutines if the variables have or have not received parameter values

```perl
if ( $email && $password ) {
    process_reset( $email, $new_password ) ;
}
else { show_password_form( ) ; }
```

4 Then, close the HTML page and database connection

```perl
print $cgi->end_html ;
$dbh->disconnect ;
```

5 Add a subroutine to display a password reset form

```perl
sub show_password_form {
    print $cgi->style('span{width:100px;display:inline-block}') ;
    print $cgi->start_form ;
    print $cgi->h2( 'Reset Your Password' ) ;
    print $cgi->p( $cgi->span( 'Email:' ) ,
            $cgi->textfield( 'email' ) ) ;
    print $cgi->p( $cgi->span( 'New Password:' ) ,
            $cgi->password_field( 'new_password' ) ) ;
    print $cgi->submit( 'Reset Password' ) ;
    print $cgi->end_form ;
}
```

6 Add a subroutine to implement a password update

```perl
sub update_password {
    my ( $email, $new_password ) = @_ ;
    my $update = $dbh->prepare(
    "UPDATE users SET password = ? WHERE email = ?") ;
    $update->execute( $new_password, $email ) ;
}
```

...continues
on the next page

...cont'd

7 Add a subroutine to check that the user is registered

```perl
sub email_exists {
    my ( $email ) = @_ ;
    my $check = $dbh->prepare(
    "SELECT COUNT(*) FROM users WHERE email = ?") ;
    $check->execute( $email ) ;
    my ( $count ) = $check->fetchrow_array ;
    return $count > 0 ;
}
```

8 Add a subroutine to assign a new password

```perl
sub process_reset {
    my ( $email, $new_password ) = @_ ;
    $new_password = sha256_hex( $new_password ) ;
    if ( email_exists( $email ) ) {
        update_password( $email, $new_password ) ;
        print $cgi->h2( 'Password reset successful!' ) ;
        print $cgi->a( { -href => 'shop-login.pl' }, 'Login' ) ;
    }
    else {
        print $cgi->h2( 'User not recognized.' ) ;
        print $cgi->a( { -href => 'shop-register.pl' },
            'Register' ) ;
    }
}
```

9 Save the file named as "shop-reset.pl" in the web server's **/htdocs** directory, then hit the "Reset Password" link on the login page to see the password reset form

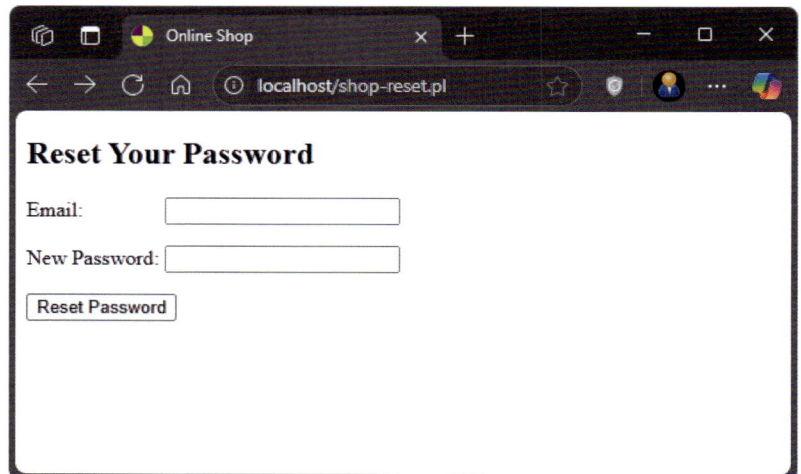

Resetting a password

1 Enter the email address of an unregistered user and a password, then hit the **Reset Password** button to see the reset attempt fail

Reset Your Password

Email: bob@example.com

New Password: ●●●●●●●●

Reset Password

User not recognized.

Register

localhost/shop-register.pl

2 Now, enter the email address of a registered user and a password, then hit **Reset Password** to see the reset attempt succeed

Reset Your Password

Email: mike@example.com

New Password: ●●●●●●●●

Reset Password

Password reset successful!

Login

localhost/shop-login.pl

Offering products

Registered users can enter their email address and password on the login page to enter the online shop on an offers page.

shop-offers.pl

1 Begin a Perl script by acquiring support, and supplying an HTTP HTML header and an HTML page title
```perl
require './shop-hdr.pl' ;
print $cgi->header( 'text/html' ) ;
print $cgi->start_html( -title => 'Online Shop' ) ;
```

2 Next, ensure that the user is logged in
```perl
my $user_id = $cgi->param( 'user_id' ) ;
if ( !$user_id ) { print $cgi->redirect( 'shop-login.pl' ) ; }
```

3 Now, gather all product item details from the database
```perl
my $sth = $dbh->prepare(
"SELECT id, name, price FROM items" ) ;
$sth->execute( ) ;
```

4 Then, begin a form to forward selected items
```perl
print $cgi->start_form(
    -method => 'POST', -action => 'shop-cart.pl' ) ;
```

5 Define a table that will display the offered items
```perl
print "<style>table{width:550px;text-align:left;}
    th{background:black;color:white;}</style>" ;
print "<table><tr><th colspan=2>Item</th>
    <th>Price \$</th><th>Quantity</th></tr>" ;
```

6 Now, populate the table cells
```perl
while ( my ($id, $name, $price) = $sth->fetchrow_array) {
    print "<tr><td>$name</td>" ;
    print "<td><img src='images/$name.png'></td>" ;
    print "<td>$price</td>" ;
    print $cgi->hidden( -name => 'user_id',
                              -value => $user_id ) ,
    $cgi->hidden( -name => "item_id_$id" ,
                              -value => $id ) ,
    $cgi->hidden( -name => "item_name_$id" ,
                              -value => $name ) ,
    $cgi->hidden( -name => "item_price_$id" ,
                              -value => $price ) ;
    print "<td>", $cgi->popup_menu(
    -name => "item_qty_$id", -values => [0..3] ) ,
    "</td></tr>" ;
}
```

...cont'd

7 End the table with a form submission button
```
print "<tr><td colspan=3></td>
    <td><input type='submit' value='View Cart'>
    </td></tr></table>" ;
```

8 Also, end the form and HTML page
```
print $cgi->end_form ;
print $cgi->end_html ;
```

9 Finally, close the database connection
```
$dbh->disconnect ;
```

10 Save the file named as "shop-offers.pl" in the web server's **/htdocs** directory, then log in and use the quantity option drop-downs to select some items

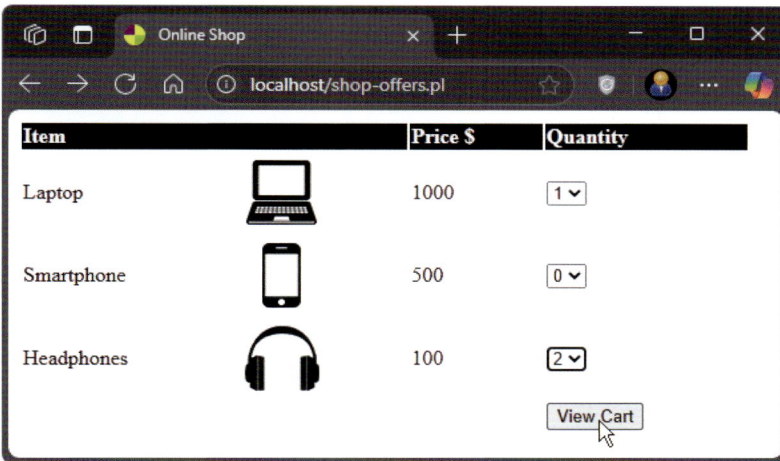

images\laptop.png
images\smartphone.png
images\headphones.png

11 Hit the **View Cart** button to submit the form and load a page where the user can review their selection

Reviewing selection

After selecting items on the offers page the use can review their selection on the cart page.

PL

shop-cart.pl

1 Begin a Perl script by acquiring support, and supplying an HTTP HTML header and an HTML page title

```perl
require './shop-hdr.pl' ;
print $cgi->header( 'text/html' ) ;
print $cgi->start_html( -title => 'Online Shop' ) ;
```

2 Next, ensure that the user is logged in

```perl
my $user_id = $cgi->param( 'user_id' ) ;
if ( !$user_id ) { print $cgi->redirect( 'shop-login.pl' ) ; }
```

3 Now, begin a form to forward selected items

```perl
print $cgi->start_form( -method => 'POST',
    -action => 'shop-checkout.pl' ) ;
```

4 Then, close the HTML page and database connection

```perl
print $cgi->end_html ;
$dbh->disconnect ;
```

5 Define a table that will display the selected items

```perl
print "<style>table { width:550px; text-align:left; }
th { background:black; color:white; }</style>" ;
print "<table><tr><th colspan=2>Item</th>
<th>Quantity</th><th>Total</th></tr>" ;
```

6 Now, call a subroutine that will create a table row for each selected item

```perl
render_rows( $user_id ) ;
```

7 End the table with a form submission button

```perl
print "<tr><td colspan=3></td>
    <td><input type='submit' value='View Cart'>
    </td></tr></table>" ;
```

8 Also, end the form and HTML page, then close the database connection

```perl
print $cgi->end_form ;
print $cgi->end_html ;
$dbh->disconnect ;
```

9 Finally, add the subroutine to create item table rows

```perl
sub render_rows {
    my ( $user_id ) = @_ ;
    my $total = 0 ;
    foreach my $key ( $cgi->param ) {
        next unless ( $key =~ /^item_qty_(\d+)$/ ) ;
        my $quantity = $cgi->param( $key ) ;
        next if $quantity == 0 ;
        my $id = $1 ;
        my $name = $cgi->param( "item_name_$id" ) ;
        my $price = $cgi->param( "item_price_$id" ) ;
        my $subtotal = $price * $quantity ;
        $total += $subtotal ;
        print "<tr><td>$name</td>" ;
        print "<td><img src='images/$name.png'></td>" ;
        print $cgi->hidden( -name => 'user_id',
                                    -value => $user_id ) ,
            $cgi->hidden( -name => "item_id_$id",
                                    -value => $id ) ,
            $cgi->hidden( -name => "item_name_$id",
                                    -value => $name ) ;
        print "<td>",
            $cgi->textfield( -name => "item_qty_$id" ,
                -value => $quantity, -readonly => 'readonly' ,
                -size => 1, -style => 'border:none' ) ,
            " @ \$", $price, " each</td>" ;
        print "<td>\$$subtotal</td></tr>";
    }
    print "<tr><td colspan=3>
        </td><td><strong>\$$total</strong></td></tr>" ;
}
```

> **Hot tip**
>
> In this step, the special Perl variable **$1** contains the numeric value captured by the regular expression. This value is appended in the interpolated strings to provide uniquely identifiable parameter names. In this case, as **item_name_1**, then **item_name_2**, etc.

10 Save the file named as "shop-cart.pl" in the web server's **/htdocs** directory, then review selected items

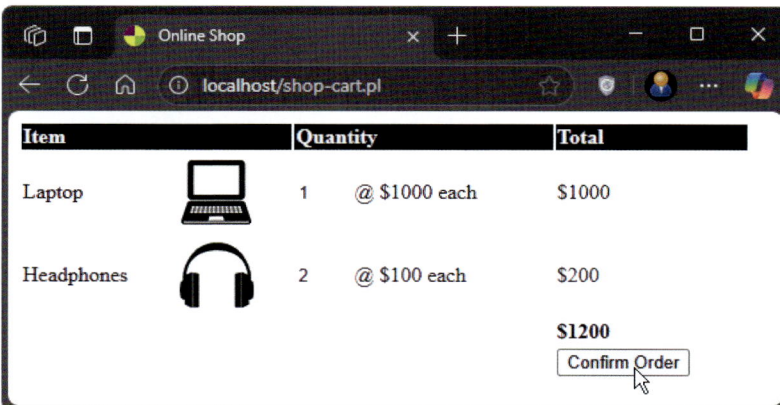

Placing orders

Having reviewed the selection on the cart page the user can proceed to confirm the order.

shop-checkout.pl

1 Begin a Perl script by acquiring support, and supplying an HTTP HTML header and an HTML page title

```perl
require './shop-hdr.pl' ;
print $cgi->header( 'text/html' ) ;
print $cgi->start_html( -title => 'Online Shop' ) ;
```

2 Next, ensure that the user is logged in

```perl
my $user_id = $cgi->param( 'user_id' ) ;
if ( !$user_id ) {
    print $cgi->redirect( 'shop-login.pl' ) ;
}
```

3 Now, output a heading and call a subroutine that will list the selected items

```perl
print $cgi->h2( 'Order Confirmation' ) ;
show_payment_form( $user_id, record_orders( $user_id ) ) ;
```

4 Then, close the HTML page and database connection

```perl
print $cgi->end_html ;
$dbh->disconnect ;
```

5 Add a subroutine to create a form that will forward the user id and selected items

```perl
sub show_payment_form {
    my ( $user_id, $item_ids_ref ) = @_ ;

    print $cgi->start_form(  -method => 'POST',
                             -action => 'shop-pay.pl' ) ;

    print $cgi->hidden( -name => 'user_id',
                -value => $user_id ) ;
    print $cgi->hidden( -name => 'item_id',
                -value => $_ ) for @$item_ids_ref ;
    print $cgi->submit( 'Make Payment' ) ;
    print $cgi->end_form ;
}
```

6 Finally, add a subroutine to record the order in the database table

```perl
sub record_orders {
    my ( $user_id ) = @_ ;
    my @collected ;

    foreach my $key ( $cgi->param ) {
        next unless $key =~ /^item_qty_(\d+)$/ ;
        my $quantity = $cgi->param( $key ) ;
        next if $quantity == 0 ;
        my $id = $1 ;
        my $item_id = $cgi->param( "item_id_$id" ) ;
        my $name = $cgi->param( "item_name_$id" ) ;

        if ( $item_id ) {
            my $sth = $dbh->prepare(
            "INSERT INTO orders (user_id, item_id, quantity)
                VALUES (?, ?, ?)" ) ;
            $sth->execute( $user_id, $item_id, $quantity )
                or die "Insert failed: $DBI::errstr" ;
            print "<p>Item: $name Quantity: $quantity</p>" ;
            push @collected, $item_id ;
        }
    }
    return @collected ;
}
```

7 Save the file named as "shop-checkout.pl" in the web server's **/htdocs** directory, then hit the **Make Payment** button to proceed

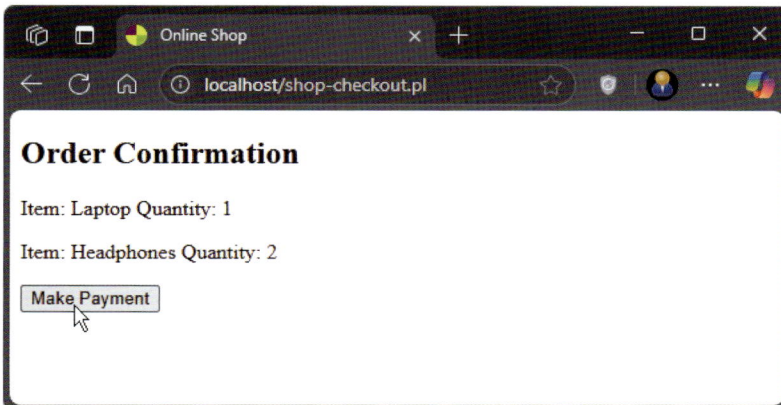

Making payment

After placing the order the user would be required to pay for the selected items via a digital payment platform such as PayPal. This example can simulate payment by displaying a dialog animation.

shop-pay.pl

1 Begin a Perl script by acquiring support, and supplying an HTTP HTML header and an HTML page title

```
require './shop-hdr.pl' ;
print $cgi->header( 'text/html' ) ;
print $cgi->start_html( -title => 'Online Shop' ) ;
```

2 Next, ensure that the user is logged in

```
my $user_id = $cgi->param( 'user_id' ) ;
if ( !$user_id ) { print $cgi->redirect( 'shop-login.pl' ) ; }
```

3 Now, call subroutines to display a dialog, update the database table for payment, and confirm success

```
show_dialog( ) ;
update_payment_status( $user_id ) ;
show_success_message( ) ;
```

4 Then, close the HTML page and database connection

```
print $cgi->end_html ;
$dbh->disconnect ;
```

5 Add a subroutine to display a dialog simulating the payment process

```
sub show_dialog {
    print $cgi->style(
        "dialog { position:fixed;top:0;left:0;margin:0; }" ) ;
    print "<dialog open>
        <img src='images/processing.gif'><br>" ;
    print $cgi->start_form( -method => 'dialog' ) ;
    print "<p style='float:right'>",
    $cgi->submit( -value => 'Complete Payment'), "</p>" ;
    print $cgi->end_form ;
    print "</dialog>";
}
```

6 Add a subroutine to confirm successful payment

```
sub show_success_message {
    print $cgi->h2( 'Payment Successful!' ) ;
    print $cgi->h3( 'You have been logged out.' ) ;
    print $cgi->p( $cgi->a( { -href => 'shop-login.pl' },
                                Return to Login' ) ) ;
}
```

...cont'd

7 Add a subroutine to update the database table
```
sub update_payment_status {
    my ( $user_id ) = @_ ;
    my $sth = $dbh->prepare(
    "UPDATE orders SET payment = 'Paid'
    WHERE payment = 'Unpaid'
    AND user_id = ? AND item_id = ?" ) ;

    foreach my $item_id ( $cgi->param( 'item_id' ) ) {
        $sth->execute( $user_id, $item_id ) ; }
}
```

8 Save the file named as "shop-pay.pl" in the web server's **/htdocs** directory then hit the **Complete Payment** button

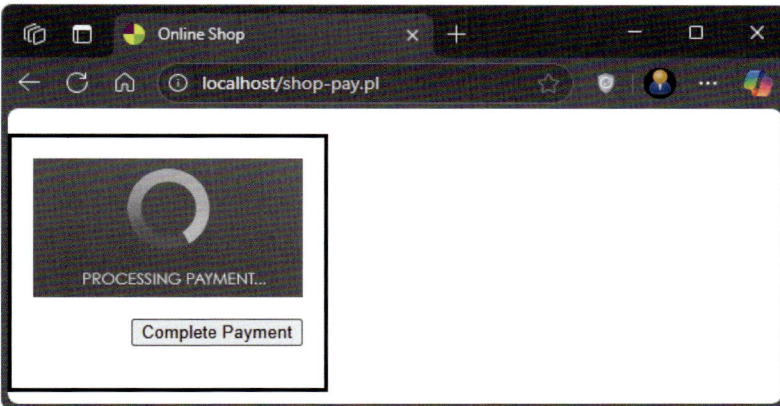

images\processing.gif

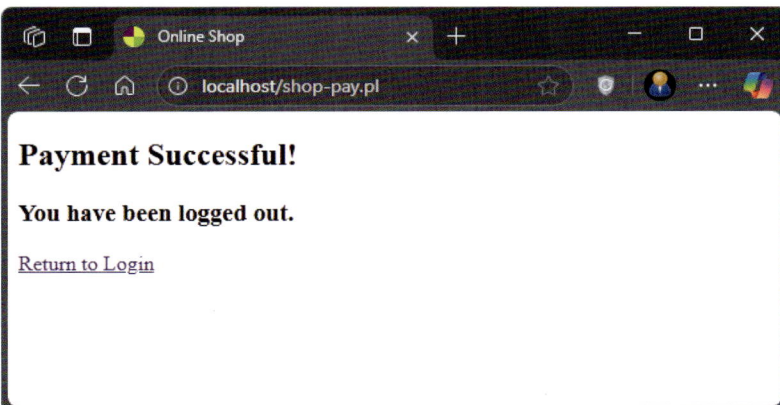

183

Payment Successful!

You have been logged out.

Return to Login

Examining sales

The website administrator can view a summary of all users and sales by examining the database contents.

shop-summary.pl

1 Begin a Perl script by acquiring support and supplying an HTTP plain text header

```perl
require './shop-hdr.pl' ;
print $cgi->header( 'text/plain' ) ;
```

2 Next, print a list of all registered users

```perl
my $sth = $dbh->prepare( "SELECT * FROM users" ) ;
$sth->execute( ) ;

print "USERS..." ;
while ( my $row = $sth->fetchrow_hashref ) {
    print "\nID: $row->{id}
        \tName: $row->{email}
        \tPassword: " . substr( $row->{password}, 0, 16 ) ;
}
$sth->finish ;
```

3 Now, print a list of all orders

```perl
print "\n\nORDERS..." ;
$sth = $dbh->prepare(
    "SELECT user_id, item_id, quantity, payment
    FROM orders
    ORDER BY user_id ;
$sth->execute( ) ;

while ( my $row = $sth->fetchrow_hashref ) {
    print "User ID: $row->{user_id}\t" ;
    print "Item: $row->{item_id}" ;
    print "Quantity: $row->{quantity}\t" ;
    print "Payment: $row->{payment}" ;
}
$sth->finish ;
```

4 Then, gather data from the three related database tables – orders (**o**), users (**u**), and items (**i**)

```perl
$sth = $dbh->prepare(
    "SELECT o.user_id, u.email, i.name AS item, o.quantity
    FROM orders o
    JOIN users u ON o.user_id = u.id
    JOIN items i ON o.item_id = i.id
    WHERE o.payment = 'Paid'
    ORDER BY o.user_id, o.item_id" ) ;
$sth->execute( ) ;
```

5 Finally, print a summary of each user's purchases, then close the database connection

```
print "\n\nSUMMARY..." ;
my %summary ;
while ( my $row = $sth->fetchrow_hashref ) {
    push @{ $summary{ $row->{user_id} }{items} },
    "$row->{quantity}x $row->{item}" ;
    $summary{ $row->{user_id} }{email} = $row->{email} ;
}

foreach my $uid ( sort keys %summary ) {
    my ( $name ) = split /@/, $summary{$uid}{email} ;
    $name = ucfirst( $name ) ;
    my $items =
        join(" and ", @{ $summary{$uid}{items} } ) ;
    print "\n\n$name purchased $items" ;
}
$dbh->disconnect;
```

6 Save the file named as "shop-summary.pl" in the web server's **/htdocs** directory, then run the program to see the online shop summary

```
localhost/shop-summary.pl          ×    +                    –    □    ×

←  C  ⌂  ⓘ  localhost/shop-summary.pl           ⊕  ☆    ⦿  ●  …

USERS...
ID: 1    Name: andy@example.com   Password: e5e0b754700cd0f3
ID: 2    Name: dave@example.com   Password: c2f33a79bee4d81e
ID: 3    Name: mike@example.com   Password: a45e2df6b898e7c4

ORDERS...
User ID: 1        Item: 2 Quantity: 3      Payment: Paid
User ID: 2        Item: 1 Quantity: 2      Payment: Paid
User ID: 3        Item: 1 Quantity: 1      Payment: Paid
User ID: 3        Item: 3 Quantity: 2      Payment: Paid

SUMMARY...
Andy purchased 3x Smartphone
Dave purchased 2x Laptop
Mike purchased 1x Laptop and 2x Headphones
```

Summary

- An online shop can use Perl's **DBI** module for database interaction, the **CGI** module for input/output, and the **Digest::SHA** module for password encryption.

- An online shop database can include tables to store **users** information, product **items**, and purchase **orders**.

- An SQL **INSERT INTO** query can be used to fill the **items** database table with product name and price.

- A login page can validate user credentials successfully, allowing them to enter the shop or provide an error message.

- A login page can also provide links allowing a new user to register, and allowing an existing user to reset their password.

- An SQL **INSERT INTO** query can be used to fill the **users** database table with user name and encrypted password.

- An SQL **UPDATE** query can be used to reset a user's password in the **users** table.

- After successfully logging in, a user can be tracked across the website by forwarding their identity in hidden form elements.

- Items selected for purchase by the user can also be forwarded in hidden form elements.

- Forwarded information is accessed on the receiving page by specifying its hidden form element's **name** as an argument to the CGI module's **param** method.

- The special Perl variable **$1** captures the numeric value from a regular expression, and this can be used in string interpolation to provide uniquely identifiable parameter names.

- An SQL **INSERT INTO** query can be used to fill the **orders** database table with user id, item id, and quantity.

- An SQL **UPDATE** query can be used to update the payment field of the orders table after payment is received.

- An SQL **SELECT** query can be used to review all items purchased by each user.

Index

191